I0797904

FARMING IS FEMALE

TWENTY WOMEN SHAKING UP THE FIELD

RACHEL SARAH

YELLOW JACKET

FOR MY DAUGHTERS, MAE AND CAMILLE.

AND TO WOMEN EVERYWHERE WHO FEED US IN SO MANY WAYS.

–RS

YELLOW JACKET
an imprint of Little Bee Books
yellowjacketreads.com
ISBN 978-1-4998-1566-5 (hc)
2 4 6 8 10 9 7 5 3 1
ISBN 978-1-4998-1567-2 (eb)

New York, NY

Designed by Sydney Hackley and Steph Stilwell

LCCN: 2024058906
Manufactured in China GGD 0625 | First Edition

For more information about special discounts on bulk purchases,
please contact Little Bee Books at sales@littlebeebooks.com.

CONTENTS

"THE LAND KNOWS YOU, EVEN WHEN YOU ARE LOST."

– ROBIN WALL KIMMERER, *BRAIDING SWEETGRASS*

The poet Camille Dungy once said: "I love a person who talks kindly to plants."

This describes my oldest daughter Mae, the person who inspired the idea for this book.

During the pandemic, Mae moved back home to attend college classes online. She rolled up to our house with all of her beautiful plants gently tucked into the backseat of the Prius she called "Greenie." She had plants of all sizes, from teensy "penny plants" to enormous Monsteras she'd been growing as seedlings.

My soon-to-be ex-husband and I tiptoed around the plants. And each other. (Yes, I'd started writing this book at the same time that I'd decided to get a divorce—during the pandemic.)

During this time, I thought a lot about what matters most in life. What was at the top of my list? Food. Every day to survive, we need to eat. We need to feed our children. Food (and water) are fundamental to our survival.

Mae told me about one of her favorite classes: Anthropology of Food and Culture. She was learning about how food is connected to your family and to your culture.

"We need neighborhood gardens everywhere," Mae said. "And these gardens have the capacity to grow the things that the people in this neighborhood eat. It's not just a matter of, 'Oh, let's grow lettuce.' But instead, what if we grow nopales (cacti) for the people who live here and cook with this ingredient?"

Note: there are more than 100 types of nopales, which are a common ingredient in Mexican dishes.

"Think about what foods are familiar to people," Mae told me. She encouraged me to interview women farmers about their stories—starting with farmers in California. So, I wrote a feature for *The Guardian* about how these farmers in California were "filling in the gaps" for food access during the pandemic.

And this book was born.

I started to read more and ask more questions. I noticed how women farmers all around the country were stepping up to feed their communities—especially during COVID.

Who grew the food that you're eating for dinner? Most kids in the United States do not know the answer to this question. Through stories based on personal interviews I did with more than thirty women around the country, I hope to answer this question for you.

Women today are at the forefront of farming in the United States. Women, on average, run smaller, more diversified farms that sell directly to people—which means that women farmers are driving local economies. (I'd initially titled this book *Move Over, Old MacDonald.* I wanted to renounce the played-out image of the American farmer as Old McDonald.)

Women have always been essential to farming but have previously been invisible. Today, women farmers in the United States are younger, more likely to be beginning farmers, and more likely to live on the farm they operate compared to male farmers.

While working on this book, I went on a few road trips to visit farms in California, Oregon, and Idaho. I witnessed in real life that food is power.

Back home, Mae and her little sister, Camille, had regular cooking parties every night. From the kitchen, music blasted, streaming with their laughter. "Dinner's ready!" one of them would call out. Some of the meals they made:

- Homemade ravioli stuffed with sweet potatoes
- Lentil soup and flatbreads
- Plantains and guacamole

Thank you to every woman and every farmer in this book—for giving me the opportunity to listen to you and to write your stories. I'm so grateful for your time and openness. And lastly, thank you for feeding and nourishing all of us.

IVY WALLS

FOUNDER: Ivy Leaf Farms

WHERE: Sunnyside, Houston, Texas

ONE WORD TO DESCRIBE: *visionary*

BEGINS HER DAY: checking this week's crops in the fields

SPECIAL SAUCE: drives a tractor!

INSTAGRAM: @IvyLeafFarms

WEBSITE: ivyleaffarms.com

PRONOUNS: she/her

Ivy Walls finished her lunch at the hospital in Houston, Texas, where she was working, and checked her phone. Then she jumped up and screamed.

"What's wrong?" one of Ivy's co-workers asked.

Without answering, Ivy kept leaping up and down. "It's Beyoncé!" Ivy held the phone to her chest.

"She's calling you?"

"She picked me!" Ivy laughed and tried to take a breath. Excitement buzzed through her like a swarm of bees.

Beyoncé —who's also from Houston—had chosen Ivy as the winner of a $10,000 grant she was giving away.

$10,000! This moment changed Ivy's life.

The money would allow Ivy to leave her current job as an infection preventionist—a person who makes sure that healthcare workers and patients are doing all the things they should to prevent infections—and set up the farm she'd dreamed about for so long.

Ivy grew up and still lived in South Houston, in a community called Sunnyside. Ivy *loved* Sunnyside. As a kid, she ran around with her brother and sister on her family's small farm. Getting in the dirt was so much fun, she says. Her first pet? Not a dog or a cat . . . it was a horse!

When COVID hit Sunnyside, everything changed. For as long as Ivy could remember, there had only been *one* grocery store in town. The pandemic made it even harder to get healthy food.

"The fruits and vegetables here were often rotting or bruised," Ivy said. "If you're not eating fresh fruit and vegetables, it can be hard to stay healthy," she explained. Many people in her community got very sick during the pandemic. Ivy wanted to change this: She wanted to nourish her community.

She'd already started a small garden in her backyard, and it was thriving. Every week, she even gave away vegetables—free!—to all her neighbors. Ivy would drive around to share her produce and ask for her neighbors' phone numbers. Ivy made the rounds every week to drop off fresh tomatoes, fruit, carrots, kale, and more.

"I would just text them and say, 'Hi, would you like some zucchini? Hi, would you like some okra?' Then I would drop it off on their doorsteps."

She spread the word on Instagram using #urbanfarmer, #Blackgirlswithplants, and #Melaningardener. "Everything I grow is free!" Ivy said.

Not surprisingly, word spread around town.

EAT LOCAL

Ivy encourages everyone to try to eat food that's grown locally. "People think that food justice has to be super radical, but it can be as simple as supporting the farmer who is growing food in your community," Ivy says.

The money from Beyoncé had come at just the right time. Ivy asked if she could expand her farm here. Ivy's dad, Walter—a computer engineer for NASA—stepped up to be his daughter's lead farmhand. Ivy drives the same tractor that her grandfather did! In fact, during the Great Depression, Ivy's grandpa delivered vegetables to *his* neighbors.

Ivy describes her community as "historically Black." This is because white politicians in Texas had segregated Sunnyside (as well as other neighborhoods in Texas) in the 1900s to mandate that Black families had to live here, separate from whites.

These same politicians prohibited Black families from buying their own homes. And they started to throw away all of their trash here in Sunnyside.

"They turned this community into a dump, with literally miles of trash," Ivy said. Some residents say that the trash seemed to reach the sky at one point.

That was not all. White leaders in Houston also installed an incinerator, which burned garbage without a filter. It spewed awful-smelling smoke and toxins into the air. One inhabitant described the incinerator as the tallest building in Sunnyside.

Even so, Black-owned businesses thrived. Some people called this stretch of Cullen Boulevard "Black Wall Street."

Texas is a state known for its oil and gas industry. Houston has become the center of the world's oil production. But in the 1980s, the price of gas started to drop as countries like Saudi Arabia and Nigeria and states like Alaska produced more oil. This affected the oil business in Texas, and many businesses in Sunnyside, including local grocery stores, shut their doors.

This is how Sunnyside started to experience "food apartheid." The term "food apartheid" describes the racist and oppressive systems that create inequitable food environments.

It's often in communities like Sunnyside that people live without access to fresh food—because white leaders segregated people, forcing them to live in neighborhoods with no grocery stores.

"DID YOU KNOW THAT 95 PERCENT OF FARMERS IN THE UNITED STATES ARE WHITE? . . . AND 64 PERCENT OF FARMERS ARE MALE?"

Nearly half of all Black-owned farms are cattle farms. Black farmers have lost 98 percent of their land over the past century due to factors that include discrimination from the United States Department of Agriculture.[1]

[1]Chloe K. Li, "How are Black American farmers reclaiming their land?" The Take by Al Jazeera, Sept. 21, 2022, https://www.aljazeera.com/podcasts/2022/9/21/how-are-black-american-farmers-reclaiming-their-land.

Fortunately, the garbage incinerator in Sunnyside closed in 1974. Ever since, local leaders have talked about what to do with this land. Hopefully, it will soon become the Sunnyside Solar Project to provide solar power to thousands of homes in and around Houston.

Thanks to Ivy, the first locally sourced grocery store and restaurant in the neighborhood opened in Sunnyside in 2022! Ivy and her friend Jeremy Peaches launched Fresh Houwse Grocery, "where we source produce from local farmers in and around Houston," said Ivy. The first week, people showed up to purchase mustard and turnip greens, collards, sweet potatoes, cabbage, and more.

In July 2024, Ivy's farm was hit by Hurricane Beryl, knocking out power to her home, along with millions of others. Hurricanes are intensifying and reaching more communities around the world as the climate warms, but Ivy and her family are resilient and recovering. "We now have our small food system built by Black urban farmers in the fourth largest city in America," said Ivy.

TAKE A FIELD TRIP TO YOUR LOCAL FARM!

All over the United States, urban communities have been reclaiming empty lots to grow food. It's easy to find one of these city gardens if you search online! Check the hours and ask your teacher and/or parent to take you to visit one.

LEAH PENNIMAN

FOUNDER: Soul Fire Farm
WHERE: Grafton, New York
ONE WORD TO DESCRIBE: *tenacious*
BEGINS HER DAY: at 5 a.m. to work out
SPECIAL SAUCE: storytelling
INSTAGRAM: @LeahPenniman
WEBSITE: soulfirefarm.org
PRONOUNS: li/she/ya/elle

As a little girl, Leah Penniman describes spending "long hours in the forested wetland, hopping from one sun-dappled mossy mound to the next, never slipping into the soggy muck, and never stepping on any rare lady slipper flowers or vibrant red-spotted newts."

She loved reading through the encyclopedias that her father had on his shelves about photosynthesis and the way that trees are "taking in our carbon dioxide and gifting us with oxygen to inhale."

In her book *Black Earth Wisdom: Soulful Conversations with Black Environmentalists*, Leah described herself and her two siblings as "three Black Kreyol children growing up in a conservative rural white town in the '80s." They "relied on this refuge" of the forested wetland.

"To say that the Ashburnham public schools were racially brutal would be an understatement. From elementary school, when we were informed by a classmate that 'brownies are not allowed in this school,' to the interminable bullying of middle- and high school, which included taunting, assaults, and one student attempting to blind me with her fingernails so that I would be 'too ugly for white boys to look at,' to the school officials' complicity with and excuses for the assault, public school was a place of terror."

Leah and her sister formed the Junior Ecologists Kids Club in elementary school, "which had exactly two members," she says. "When we could not convince our elementary school to start a recycling program, we put out our own bins and dragged home aluminum cans on the school bus to rinse in our backyard and redeem. We went on 'pollution patrol' with our blue Huffy bicycles, picking up garbage, placing our bodies between loggers and trees, and guerilla planting the denuded medians in the road."

Leah is referring to barren strips of land between the lanes of opposing traffic that you see when you're driving on the highway or freeway that, if planted, can lower emissions.

Leah adds: "We wrote original anthems and spoken word poems, and sang these praise lyrics to the forest. Perhaps most ambitiously, we researched long lists of actions people could take to protect the environment, and handwrote this advice on hundreds of postcards that we sent to people listed in the phone book. Naima and I made a solemn covenant with the wild animals and plants, pledging allegiance to the earth with these words, 'We will never forget how to listen to you; we will always stand with you.'"

In high school, Leah started working every summer at different farms near her home. This was where she felt liberated. She'd even saved up enough money to attend some local farming conferences. But time and time again, she was surrounded by people who did not look like her. Everyone who stepped on the stage to speak was white.

Leah dreamed of having her own farm one day, but she wasn't sure how she could make this happen on her own. So, when Leah went to the Northeast Organic Farming Association conference at age nineteen, she had a plan.

Leah showed up with a small stack of handmade business cards on slips of paper. She walked around and handed them out to anyone who appeared Black, Latine, or Indigenous.

"Hi," she said. "I'm Leah Penniman. I'm wondering if you might have a few minutes to chat with me?"

One by one, people said, "Yes."

Leah started building a community with others committed to justice in the food system.

In college, Leah majored in environmental science and went on to teach high school science for seventeen years. In 2010, her family started Soul Fire Farm, "an Afro-Indigenous centered community farm dedicated

to uprooting racism and seeding sovereignty in the food system through our emphasis on farmer training, feeding folks who lack access to life-giving food, and rabble-rousing for systems change."

BIPOC FARMERS LEFT BEHIND

Ximena Bustillo is a multi-platform reporter at *NPR* covering politics and policy in Washington and has been writing about Black farmers in the United States for years.

Before joining *NPR*, she was an award-winning food and agriculture policy reporter and newsletter author at *POLITICO* covering immigration, climate, labor, supply chain and equity issues.

One topic Ximena has written about is how Black farmers have struggled to get loans—or money—from the USDA for their farms.

The USDA stands for the United States Department of Agriculture—it's the government agency that's responsible for developing and executing federal laws related to farming and food. (It was founded by President Abraham Lincoln in 1862!)

What this means is that the USDA has "discriminated against Black farmers resulting in uneven distribution of farm loans and assistance. This caused many Black farmers to lose their land and farms to foreclosure," Ximena writes. "Black farmers still receive the lowest amount of loans."

Today, *everyone* in the farming space across the United States seems to know who Leah is. People all over the world know her as a persevering leader. She walked into the white-dominated space—the world of farming in the United States—to write a new narrative.

"Black land matters," Leah writes in her first book, *Farming While Black*. This is why she aspires to empower Brown and Black farmers to regain "food sovereignty," which means "the right of peoples to healthy and culturally appropriate food produced through ecologically sound and sustainable methods, and their right to define their own food and agriculture systems. It puts the aspirations and needs of those who produce, distribute, and consume food at the heart of food systems and policies rather than the demands of markets and corporations." Leah attributes this idea to the Declaration of Nyéléni, which was the first global forum on food sovereignty. "White neighborhoods have an average of four times as many supermarkets as predominantly Black communities."

BLACK LAND MATTERS

A typical day for Leah begins with a 5 a.m. (!) morning run, and then back to her home office to start her workday. "We built this passive solar home and it was the only building here for the first ten years. So it has many functions, with offices, a kitchen, and a gathering space."

This is where Leah wrote her second book, *Black Earth Wisdom*, a series of conversations with thirty Black environmentalists, to explore the relationship between people of color and nature. Soul Fire Farm is also where Leah raised her two children, Emet and Neshima, with her husband, Jonah.

Afternoons find Leah out on the farm with the Soul Fire team: seeding, transplanting plants, or harvesting. She talks about her time out there as "glorious and authentic." This is her happy place—in the field with her team. "To free ourselves, we must feed ourselves!" is something Leah often says.

But Leah does a lot more than farm. Teaching is one of her true loves; she loved—and still does!—to lead students out to the land to learn. "I think that teaching on the wall is wall-less teaching," she said. "It's so much more fun to go into the forest!" Every day, she mentors a new generation of activist farmers so they can go back home and farm for their communities.

That's why, every year, people come from all over the world to work and learn at Soul Fire Farm. "What brings deep satisfaction is seeing the impact that our alumni are having across the nation and even internationally," said Leah. "Ultimately, it's not about what Soul Fire is doing, right? It's about feeding this movement and growing this movement."

SUZANNE WILLOW & LANITA WITT

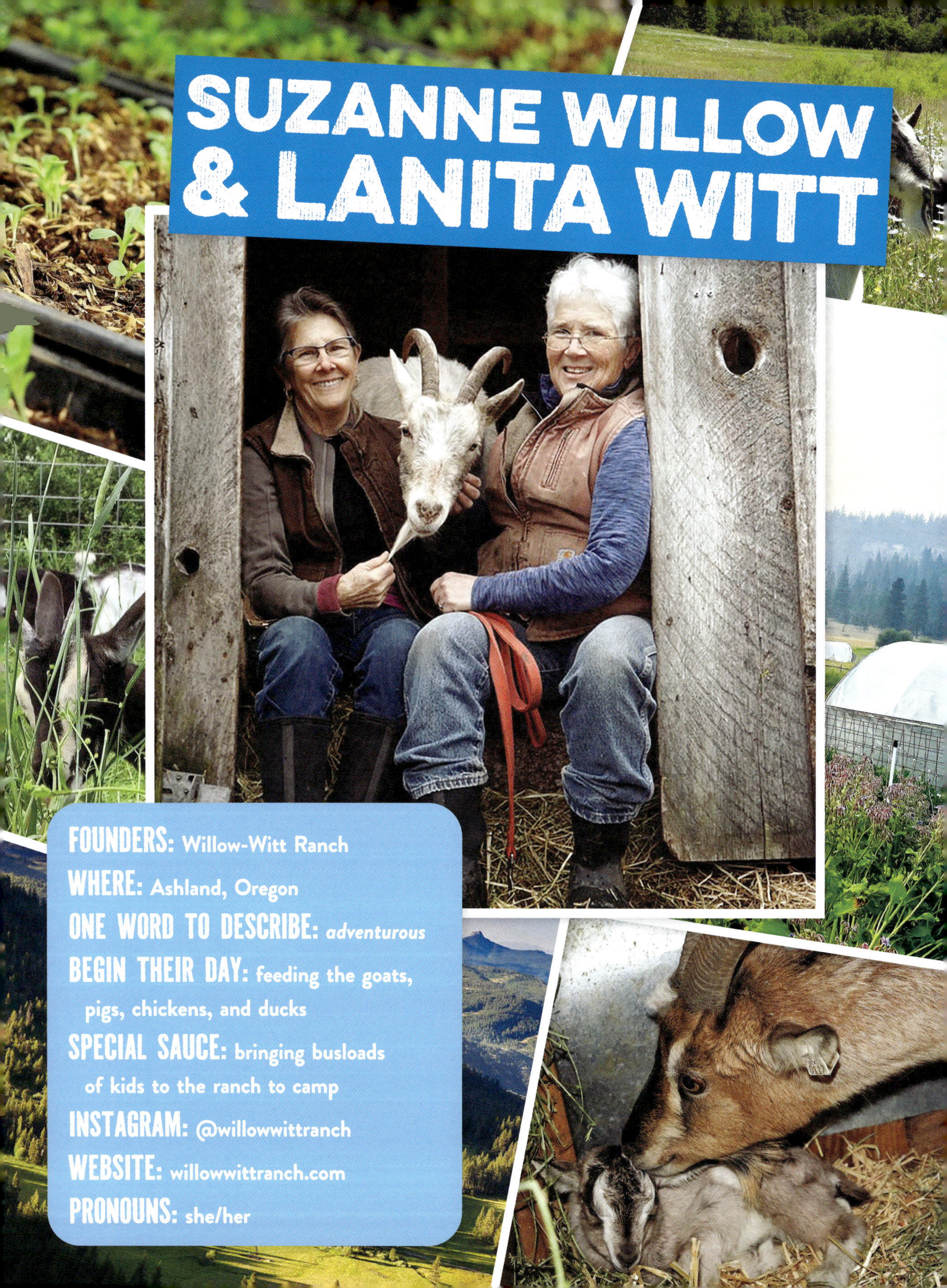

FOUNDERS: Willow-Witt Ranch

WHERE: Ashland, Oregon

ONE WORD TO DESCRIBE: *adventurous*

BEGIN THEIR DAY: feeding the goats, pigs, chickens, and ducks

SPECIAL SAUCE: bringing busloads of kids to the ranch to camp

INSTAGRAM: @willowwittranch

WEBSITE: willowwittranch.com

PRONOUNS: she/her

"Stop!" Brooke called out as her mothers drove up a dirt road outside of Ashland, Oregon. "Look down there at that beautiful valley!"

Eight-year-old Brooke bounced up and down in the back seat and pointed out the window to the **For Sale** sign.

Brooke's mothers, Lanita Witt and Suzanne Willow, had dreamed about buying a small piece of land to raise their daughter. Forty acres. That's what they were dreaming of—somewhere near a good school district for their daughter.

But this **For Sale** sign said it was 445 acres!

Even so, these two adventurous mothers decided to drive up snowy Shale City Road on that sparkling morning on New Year's Eve, 1984.

"Driving toward a mapped parcel, we looked down into a beautiful valley with a big barn and little house under four feet of snow, and thought about the family that lived there—in summer!" recalls Suzanne.

The road led to a meadow shaped in the letter *T*. Trees loomed in every direction. "Two weeks later, we skied into the valley with the big barn and the little house, and put in an offer," says Suzanne. "The rest, as they say, is history."

Lanita and Suzanne put down $5,000 to become the owners of this massive property in the Southern Oregon Cascade mountains; eventually, they paid $400,000 for the land.

"At the edge of the meadow was the roof of a house and a big barn," is how Lanita remembered the land the first time she explored their new home. That first winter, the snow buried their home!

"Just keep your good jobs in town," Lanita's mom told them. Neither woman had ever farmed before!

Lanita was a doctor who cared for women and their babies during pregnancy and childbirth. Suzanne was a primary care physician assistant. Over the next year, they both found new jobs in Oregon and started their journey to restore the land. That first year was not easy. "We didn't have a phone for six years," says Suzanne.

Their tomato plants froze because it was so cold. Both women cried and asked, "Have we moved to the north pole?" The land was also so dry it couldn't even hold water. They noticed the trees looked sickly, but knew nothing about trees, so they called a local forester named Marty. Maybe he could teach them about the foliage on their land.

When Marty arrived, Suzanne and Lanita showed him a small piece of paper that had been taped in the cupboard of the house by a previous owner. It said:

**LIVE LIKE YOU'RE GOING TO DIE TOMORROW;
FARM LIKE YOU'RE GOING TO LIVE FOREVER.**

They told Marty this was their dream: to live like they're going to die tomorrow, and to farm like they're going to live forever.

"He walked the land and then sat us down at the kitchen table," said Lanita. "In his quiet matter-of-fact way, he announced, 'Well, ladies, you have a mighty sick forest.'"

Marty started cutting down the diseased and dying trees that were sick thanks to years of logging. But the land also had potholes from the cattle that had grazed in the meadows for more than 150 years. They'd destroyed the soil. Suzanne and Lanita knew that if the grass was ever going to come up again, they had to keep the cows out. So they put up fences and planted over 15,000 native willows.

Amazingly, flowers started to grow. And grow. Today, Sand Hill Cranes swoop over the fields with multitudes of butterflies.

"Fresh water runs off the land throughout the summer," said Lanita.

"The gullies are healing with grassy bottoms and the meadows are soggy as they should be."

Also, much to everyone's surprise, the Western Pond Turtles, a threatened species, found their way up to the cold spring-fed pond at Willow-Witt Ranch. Today, they are thriving there.

The two women share a good laugh about what they call "not such good ideas" over the years. For example, they purchased five Cashmere goats, and soon, the goats had *so* many babies, there were a hundred goats roaming around!

Lanita and Suzanne decided to shear, or cut, the soft Cashmere wool to sell it. But they didn't make a lot of money that way. So they decided to sell the goats for meat instead. They also trained the male goats to carry their gear on long hikes, and the female goats gave them "raw fresh milk" which they sold around town.

"Goats are some of the best people we know," Lanita said. "We hand-raise the babies so they learn manners. They don't butt people with their heads or jump on them."

If you visit Willow-Witt Ranch today, one of the first things you'll see alongside the road is a sign called **The History of This Land**. It's a map that starts out 22 million years ago by showing you the first volcanic activity in the area. It leads you to how the Indigenous people—upland Takelma, Shasta, and Athapaskan—cared for this land. They cultivated the purple edible wildflowers (called Camas) here and dug up the roots for food.

"Indigenous people lived here for more than 8,000 years," Lanita says, explaining that she and Suzanne have worked with local tribes to restore their practices here.

One summer, a teenager was visiting the ranch, and he asked if the goats' pee came from the same place their milk did. That's when Lanita and Suzanne knew it was time to teach young people about where food came from, "like how milk gets into the jar."

They opened up their ranch to school visits and summer camps. They built large tents with bunk beds for kids to stay for a week with their teachers. Kids wandered through the forest to find bugs and flowers, feed the goats, and pick veggies from the garden.

A few years ago, Lanita felt a pain in her stomach. She knew something wasn't right.

It was terminal cancer. She and Suzanne got busy. They wanted to protect this land for the future—especially for kids. And they did just that by getting legal protection to conserve it through the Pacific Forest Trust.

On December 15, 2022, Suzanne lay next to Lanita at home and held her hand. They'd been married for forty-three years and loved each other deeply.

"She was an amazingly smart, inventive, and capable person who could do just about whatever she put her mind to," Suzanne said.

A DAY IN THE LIFE OF A RANCHER

Write a story or a journal entry about what a day in the life would be like if you were a rancher like Suzanne and Lanita. Add illustrations and drawings. Feel free to add dialogue.

What time would you wake up?

Who would need to eat first?

How would you take care of the animals?

What would you grow on the farm?

SAARA NAFICI

DIRECTOR: Red Hook Farms

WHERE: Red Hook, Brooklyn, NY

ONE WORD TO DESCRIBE: *intentional*

BEGINS HER DAY: Getting her kids ready for school: making breakfast, packing lunches, checking backpacks. Once they're off to school, she can turn on "her farm brain."

SPECIAL SAUCE: showing up as a Mama Bear to all

INSTAGRAM: @RedHookFarms

WEBSITE: https://rhicenter.org/red-hook-farms/the-farms/

PRONOUNS: she/her

“I am the daughter of immigrants from Iran,” says Saara Nafici. “My parents came to the US two months before I was born, and I traveled through four countries in utero. During the early years of my life, I always felt somewhat unsettled.”

For most of her life, Saara says, she has asked herself questions like, “Why are we here in this country? Why are we far from our land? Now that I am here, who was here before me?”

Perhaps it’s this experience that steered Saara to seek grounding in farming, as well as the empathy to understand the young people who arrive at Red Hook Farms every week. Red Hook is a neighborhood in Brooklyn, New York, that has lacked access to affordable and healthy foods for decades.

“Most young people here are leaving the neighborhood for work in retail or fast-food chains,” Saara says. “At their jobs, no one is asking them what their goals are, how they’re feeling, what they’re thinking, or what their place in the world might be.”

So Saara, the Director of Red Hook Farms, steps in to do just that along with a dedicated team of educators and farmers. She landed at Red Hook Farms when she was three months pregnant with her first child, stepping into this incredible youth-centered urban agriculture and food justice program on one of Brooklyn’s largest farms. (Red Hook Farms is located on public land that belongs to the New York City Park’s Department and the New York City Housing Authority.)

THE LENAPE PEOPLE LIVED ALONG THE MARSHES OF THIS LAND THEY CALLED *SASSIAN*.

When the Dutch invaded this land in 1636, they pushed the Lenape out of their homes and renamed this area "Red Hook" because of the color of the soil and the shape of the land on the peninsula projecting into New York Bay.

Today, you will see shipyards and docks here from the early 1900s when this was a thriving shipping community. It's where Dell's Maraschino cherry factory and the Snapple factory used to call home. Now there's a big IKEA and a Fairway.

This neighborhood is currently home to the Red Hook Houses, the largest housing project in Brooklyn. New York City owns this housing project—it means that the government is supporting people with lower incomes to have a home. There are twenty buildings in total, with more than 6,000 people living in them.

When Hurricane Sandy struck New York City in 2012, many families in Red Hook had to evacuate. Homes and businesses flooded. There was no power for days. Some of the roads and bridges were damaged. Red Hook has been working to rebuild.

Saara often asks young people who come to Red Hook Farms: "What is the soil that I'm standing on? Who touched it before? What happened here?"

"My family three generations back was nomadic, and there is a strong connection to food in the Iranian community," Saara says. "Food is your culture. That is how you express your culture and how you pass on your culture."

Growing food has always grounded Saara. She got a degree in Conservation and Resources Studies from UC Berkeley, and the New York City Food Policy Center at Hunter College profiled her as a rising star in Food Policy.[1]

[1]Cather, "40 Under 40: The Rising Stars in New York City Food Policy," Hunter College NYC Food Policy Center, May 19, 2017, https://www.nycfoodpolicy.org/2017-40-40/.

“I’ve worked in school, community, and botanic gardens for many years, so the journey of getting here was steadily building my practice as an educator-farmer one green space at a time,” Saara says. More than anything, Saara wants Red Hook Farms to be a safe space where young people can nourish their minds, bodies, and souls.

FOOD IS YOUR CULTURE. THAT IS HOW YOU EXPRESS YOUR CULTURE AND HOW YOU PASS ON YOUR CULTURE.

“The farms are the ultimate outdoor classrooms,” Saara says. “There are no desks and no walls. This allows for incredibly expansive and meaningful conversations.” She laughs when she recalls bringing her young children to the farm as she worked. “There were times when my kids took naps in harvest crates.” When they woke up, she’d say, “Here’s a pile of dirt; off you go.”

While Saara respects the struggles of mothers who farm, she wishes our society was less punishing and more supportive of new parents. “Still, looking back on those times, I do feel proud. I did that.”

Saara has been at Red Hook Farms now for nearly a decade. Before this, she worked with youth gardening and bicycle-based programs in the SF Bay Area and Boston. She also ran a teen apprentice program at Brooklyn Botanic Garden.

Her days begin with getting her two kids ready for elementary school. “In the morning, my brain is not switched to work yet,” she laughs. Once Saara reaches one of the two farms she manages in Red Hook and strolls past the chickens and beehives, she comes alive.

She wants the farm youth to feel pride in their work. "We are stewards of a space that belongs to everyone, but also really to no one because the land belongs to itself."

"I want our young people to walk out of here—and anyone who works at the farms to walk out of here—to go into any workplace knowing their value, their worth, and their power," Saara says.

She advocates for young people here to speak up and ask questions. "Plan your work, work your plan," she often says, quoting Dead Prez. "It means coming from a space of care and intention. Looking out for your colleagues and comrades."

Saara encourages everyone to share their cultures and practices with each other on the farms and to see themselves as co-creators in this space. "For example, we have community farmers who are from different parts of China. The trellising techniques they use are super creative and resourceful."

This collaborative approach is also why she loves working with middle and high schoolers, as they can so often be more open and curious than adults. "We can all say, 'Wow, what's that? Let's figure it out together.'"

Saara adds that many people in Red Hook have faced—and continue to face—systematic racism in this community, such as a lack of public transportation, grocery stores, and affordable housing.

"Our youth deserve more. I truly believe that if every single young person had a connection to the land, to food, and to their community that our entire society would be transformed."

Saara says that farming "under capitalism and white supremacy is forever our greatest challenge." She loves to recite this line by the Afrofuturist writer Octavia E. Butler:

"THERE IS NOTHING NEW UNDER THE SUN, BUT THERE ARE NEW SUNS."

It reminds her of the infinite possibilities in our communities and in our world.

"There's so much to do in Red Hook," she says. "It's so important to connect. And to feel inspired to act."

Between June to November every year—when the farm is bursting with fruit and veggies—families can swing by Red Hook Farms to pick up fresh, local produce, such as kale, collard greens, bok choy, peppers, and more.

"Growing your own food is one of the most empowering things you can do with others," Saara says. "The farms are a place where you never stop learning. It's just a beautiful space to live and to grow in."

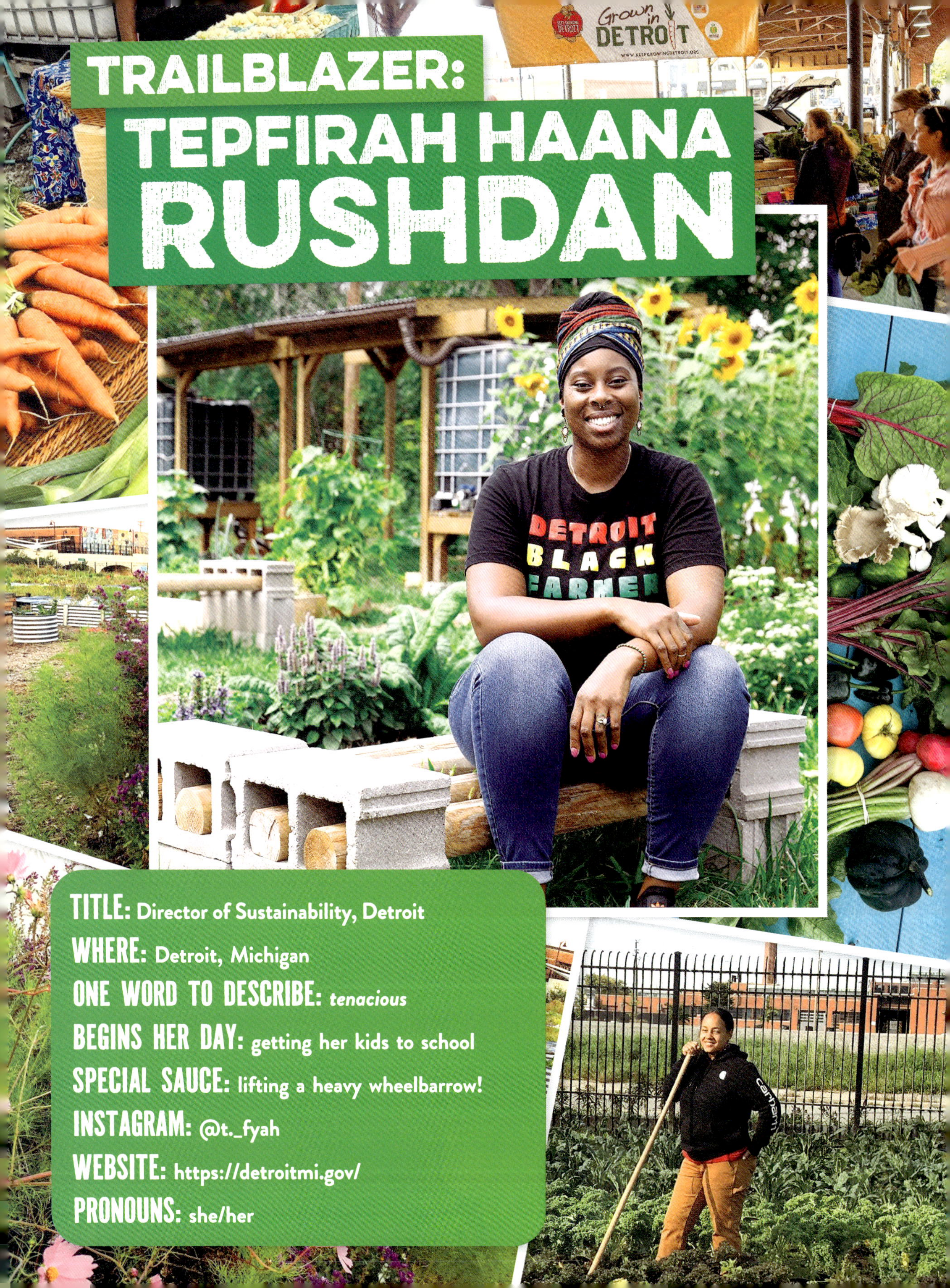

TRAILBLAZER: TEPFIRAH HAANA RUSHDAN

TITLE: Director of Sustainability, Detroit

WHERE: Detroit, Michigan

ONE WORD TO DESCRIBE: *tenacious*

BEGINS HER DAY: getting her kids to school

SPECIAL SAUCE: lifting a heavy wheelbarrow!

INSTAGRAM: @t._fyah

WEBSITE: https://detroitmi.gov/

PRONOUNS: she/her

One of the first things you might notice about Tepfirah (pronounced *Tep-Fear-Uh*) Haana Rushdan is the tattoo on her wrist. It's one word—decolonize—and it illustrates her deep roots in Detroit's urban farming and activist communities.

Tepfirah, also known as "Tee," tells the story about a recent blackout in her community, which lasted a few days without electricity or water. "I'm a woman raising kids, and I watched all of the grocery stores in Detroit empty out in one day, like they did during COVID."

During this time, she was strolling through her neighborhood, "where there are at least twenty vacant lots and all the things that come with that, like people dumping things. The city often isn't able to maintain these lots. There are hazards right here where I'm raising my children."

Tee, who's the mother of four children, says that this was an eye-opening "moment of vulnerability." She asked herself: What if the city cleans up these vacant lots and turns them into community gardens? She pictured vegetables and herbs growing, reaching up to the sun.

Tee took charge. She reached out to neighbors, formed a block club, cleaned up a few of the lots, and planted food for the community. Many neighborhoods were experiencing the same thing but struggling to purchase the gardens they were tending from the city.

Tee and three other Black women agriculturalists in Detroit—who describe themselves as "committed to the right relationship with land," combined forces to support Black farmers in Detroit. Their mission? "To purchase vacant land in one of America's Blackest cities" in order to garden and feed their communities. Tee estimates 80-85 percent of Detroit's population is Black, a figure backed up by the US Census.[1]

[1]"Detroit city, Michigan," QuickFacts, US Census Bureau, accessed March 5, 2025, https://www.census.gov/quickfacts/fact/table/detroitcitymichigan/PST045224.

THE DETROIT BLACK FARMER LAND FUND DECLARES:

"We are grounded in the historical plight of our ancestors, the last link in the chain of our struggle to reclaim not just the land that held them but our heritage. The seeds that they sowed, the soil that they touched, and the stories that they told, too, run with the land. We fight for ourselves and on behalf of the thousands of Black farmers—our ancestors and elders—who lost their land in the pursuit of our continued survival . . . We are smashing the narrative that the 'best use' of vacant land is based on financial worth alone."

Tee recognizes that Detroit is in a unique situation: 30 percent of the city's urban land is vacant and the land is relatively cheap. In other similar cities such as Cleveland, Philadelphia, and Chicago, land is much more expensive.

While many developers imagine this vacant land becoming, say, high-rise apartments or hotels, Tee points out that agriculture is "definitely development. It's just a different type of development for communities."

On Juneteenth 2020, Tee and her co-founders officially founded their organization: the Detroit Black Farmer Land Fund (@detroitblackfarmerlandfund). They had a goal to raise $5,000, and in the end, they raised $60,000. So far, this has allowed more than sixty Detroiters to purchase their own land.

"For Black people, land is the battlefield," Tee says. "A lot of issues that we see today [are] because of land theft and people being removed from their land. I think reconnecting to the land is righting the wrongs."

In just four years, these women and their communities cleaned up almost fifteen acres of vacant lots in Detroit and turned them into gardens. Tee's vision—that this is a great era for Black farmers in Detroit to purchase land—is spot-on.

In 2023, Tee was hired to be Detroit's new Director of Urban Agriculture. In the United States, only a handful of cities have a similar role. When Detroit's city leaders announced the news, the crowd erupted in loud cheers. Everyone was ecstatic.

Detroit City Planner Kathryn Underwood said about Tee: "She has a quiet demeanor, but don't be fooled . . . she will speak truth to power."

She already has. In just over six months, Tee got promoted to become Detroit's Director of the Office of Sustainability and planned a new initiative to transition to solar power in eight Detroit neighborhoods.

One proposal involves converting 250 acres of vacant land into solar farms that could provide renewable energy for the city. About her work, Tee said: "Detroiters are creative and resilient, and I believe we have real potential to become a national leader in municipal sustainability."

When she's not in her office, Tee farms in her home backyard. She grows greens, sweet potatoes, and herbs. She loves hearing the birds chirp. "I do things with my body that people label as 'man work'," she says. "Like lifting a wheelbarrow and driving a big truck."

Tee says that it's so important to know how your food gets to you, from the land to the grocery store. "When you're caring for land, out there, in it, you care about what happens to the land and what people can do on the land. . . . Don't be afraid to start farming," Tee tells people who live in cities. "Just do it! If you try to wait until you know everything, you won't start. Get out there and be open to learning."

START A GARDEN ON YOUR WINDOWSILL

"Don't be scared to grow something in your own backyard, or on your balcony, or your windowsill," Ivy says.

Green onions are a great place to start. When you buy green onions—also called scallions or spring onions—they have a root at the end that you cut off before using the green stalks and white bulb. This root is what you can regrow over and over to have a boundless supply of green onions!

STEPS TO REGROW GREEN ONIONS

YOU WILL NEED:

- -A STARTER BUNCH OF GREEN ONIONS
- -FRESH WATER
- -A JAR

STEP 1:

Have an adult help you cut off the ends of the bulbs, leaving the roots attached.

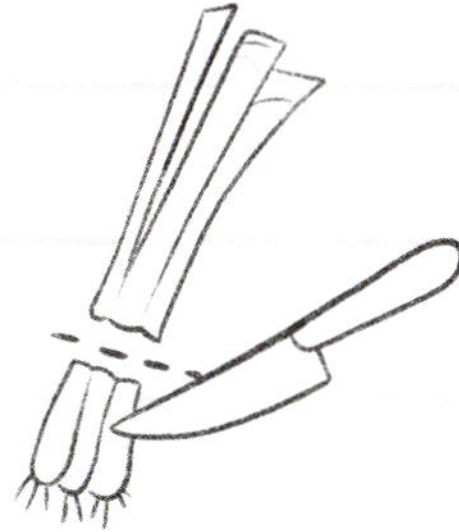

STEP 2:

Stand up the bulbs root-end down in a small jar.

STEP 3:

Add enough water to cover the roots but leave the top edges above water.

STEP 4:

Set the jar on a windowsill and keep the roots watered every day.

STEP 5:

After a few days, you will see some green shoots risc up from thc tops of thc bulbs.

STEP 6:

Change the water in the jar every two to three days.

STEP 7:

You can also transfer the onion roots to soil and continue to grow them.

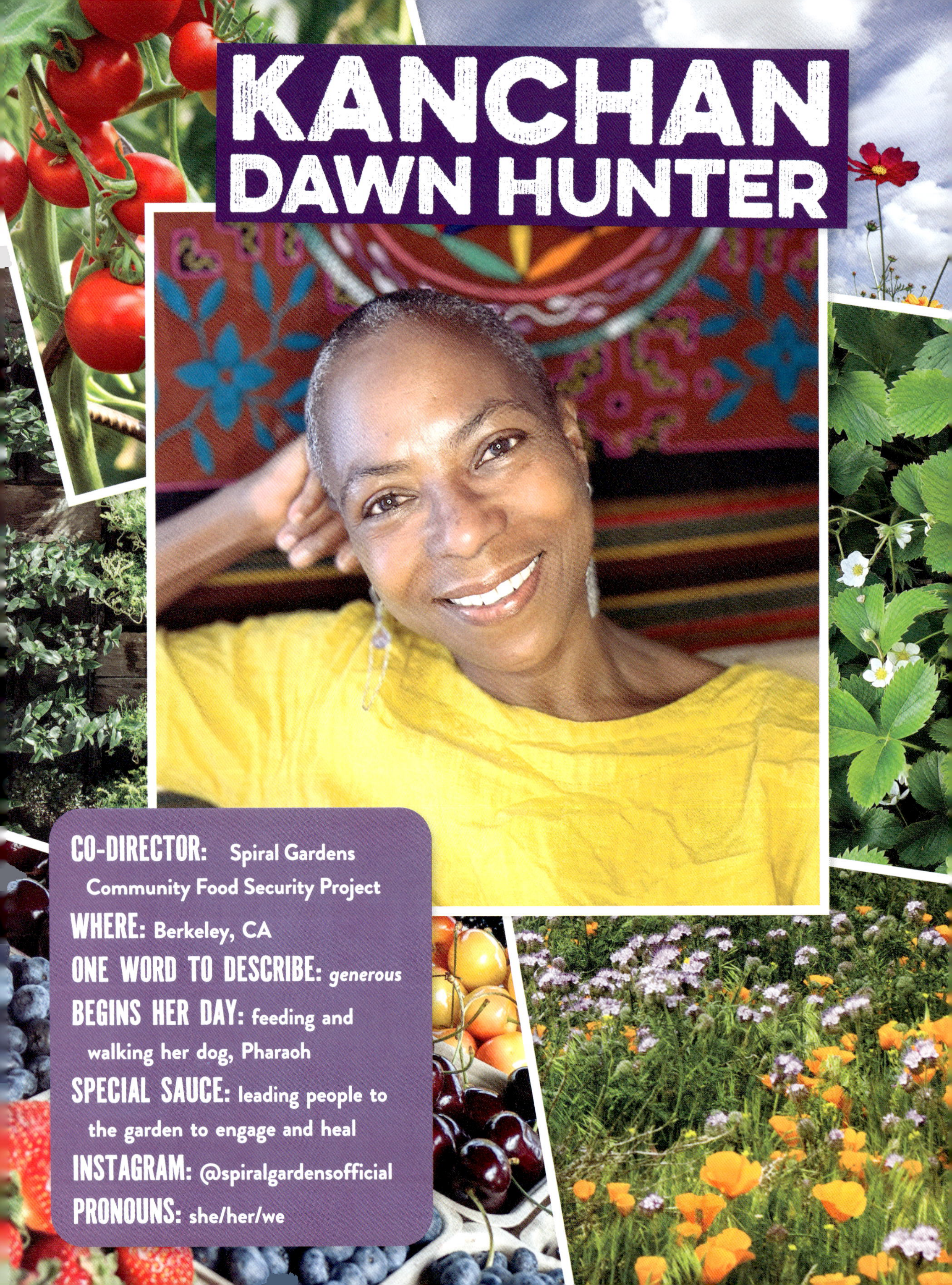

KANCHAN DAWN HUNTER

CO-DIRECTOR: Spiral Gardens Community Food Security Project

WHERE: Berkeley, CA

ONE WORD TO DESCRIBE: *generous*

BEGINS HER DAY: feeding and walking her dog, Pharaoh

SPECIAL SAUCE: leading people to the garden to engage and heal

INSTAGRAM: @spiralgardensofficial

PRONOUNS: she/her/we

It was a beautiful Sunday morning in Berkeley, California, as Kanchan Dawn Hunter drove along a busy road, headed to work at Spiral Gardens. That's when she spotted a tiny black kitten in the middle of Sacramento Avenue. Cars veered. Someone honked.

Kanchan pulled over, jumped out of her car, and scooped up the small kitty. "When I found her, I was surprised at just how ready she was to be held," Kanchan said. "She fell asleep in my hand. She was like, *I'm not going anywhere.*"

That night, Kanchan stayed up late to feed, play with, and snuggle the kitten. Its purr was a little motor. This story pretty much sums up who Kanchan is.

Love is the law is how Kanchan signs all of her emails. And it's how she lives her life.

LOVE IS THE LAW

Kanchan is a community organizer and educator. She's an herbalist and farmer, and she's also the proud Black single mother of three children. Three decades ago, Spiral Gardens was an empty lot. Some people called this block in South Berkeley an "eyesore." The Santa Fe Railroad line used to run diagonally through here to Oakland, but when people started to drive cars, the trains stopped. This space had been empty ever since.

But that's not all. There were no grocery stores with fresh fruit and vegetables in this part of Berkeley.

"It was hard to find a head of lettuce here to save your life," one neighbor said. Kanchan had a vision. She wanted to transform this barren space into an oasis.

First, she and a group of neighbors reclaimed, or took over, a small corner of land here to nourish the soil and plant seeds. Within months, they had a thriving garden.

Kanchan would knock on doors in the neighborhood and ask, "Hey, do you know about us? Guess what? There's a bunch of strawberries growing over in the garden." She pointed to the garden, leading the way to neighbors.

Even so, these two long blocks of an old, fenced-off railroad bed continued to sit vacant for years and years. A few years later, Kanchan and the neighbors knew they could grow an even bigger urban garden for the community—if they could get permission to do so.

So she and other community members went to the city of Berkeley with a proposal: Let us garden here. We'll give away fresh vegetables. We'll also provide a space for people to learn how to start their own gardens. They knocked on more doors. They went to city council meetings. And their proposal passed!

"I made it my solemn word to foster community in this space that the city of Berkeley granted us," Kanchan said. "It was a promise I made."

Today, Spiral Gardens extends into two thriving plots in Berkeley. There's a nursery where you can buy plants, a community farm with fresh veggies, and a produce stand. One volunteer here referred to it as "the secret garden."

Bees buzz around the strawberries. Every week, young people show up to volunteer. Kanchan shows them which flowers they can eat, and which plants sting. "The Earth is offering us so much, all of the time," she said. "It's what I love, and I want to share."

WHAT WOULD YOU DO WITH A VACANT LOT?

Choose one of the following ideas—or come up with your own! Write and/or draw your vision.

- Build a tiny home. What will it look like on the inside and outside?
- Plant a community garden. What will you grow there?
- Plant trees. Will you have trails? Who will come and explore?
- Create a skate park. How will you design the ramps? Who will show up to skate?
- Create a solar or wind farm. Many places in the US are ideal for either solar panels or wind turbines, which are renewable energies! What's ideal for your region?

DO YOU KNOW THE BLACK PANTHERS?

Today, all Californian public schools provide free breakfast to kids. Many kids depend on this first meal to start the day, and we have the Black Panthers to thank for paving the way.

In 1966, Huey Newton and Bobby Seale founded the Black Panther Party to document and challenge acts of police brutality against Black people in California. The Party's mission later expanded to support Black communities in many ways. It can be hard to focus at school when you're hungry, the Black Panthers knew this.

At this time, the United States government did little to help low-income Black families, so a local dancer named Ruth Beckford stepped up to co-found the "Free for Children Breakfast Program" in Oakland, California.

AT THIS TIME, THE UNITED STATES GOVERNMENT DID LITTLE TO HELP LOW-INCOME BLACK FAMILIES

Ruth mapped out a healthy, delicious menu that would feed children. She did so in a big kitchen and dining hall that passed health inspections. On the first day, 11 children came to eat. By the end of the week, 135 children showed up in the morning for Oakland's Free Breakfast Program. The program took off and communities across the country were soon feeding children breakfast before school.

H. NIETO-FRIGA

FOUNDER: SupplyChange

WHERE: Kingston, New York

ONE WORD TO DESCRIBE: *tenacious*

BEGINS HER DAY: snuggling with her wife, Madeleine

SPECIAL SAUCE: can simplify the most complex problems

INSTAGRAM: @hframz

WEBSITE: Supplychange.co

PRONOUNS: H. uses she/her professionally, and other pronouns in her personal life

"I am not a good gardener," H. Nieto-Friga confessed with a laugh.

That said, H. has one of the most important professions in the farming world: "I am the bridge between the farmer and the buyer." And she's one of maybe only "a handful" or "a small group of people in the United States who has a similar job."

In other words, she founded a company that connects small farms to the companies that buy their food—like schools, hospitals, parks, and universities.

"I'm working on a project right now to connect a woman-led Indigenous farm with the Grand Canyon National Park, just several miles away from their farm," H. says, as an example.

"It's wild how tricky it is to make this connection work." You might recognize some of the big companies H. has worked with, such as Google, Whole Foods, and Stanford University.

"I had the idea about this business since I went to grad school," H.

says. Again and again, she saw large companies try to purchase food from small farmers, but without someone to negotiate the deal, these companies "inadvertently ended up creating more harm for farmers who have suffered enough in our food system."

"All food systems are relationship-based—you need to have positive relationships, deep connections, or a large network. I act like a bridge in a lot of ways—also between ethnicities and between genders. It feels like home every time I make these connections, pulling on a web of relationships and trust that I've built."

ALL FOOD SYSTEMS ARE RELATIONSHIP-BASED—YOU NEED TO HAVE POSITIVE RELATIONSHIPS, DEEP CONNECTIONS, OR A LARGE NETWORK.

After graduating from college, H. managed a couple of farmers markets and also worked in government food policy. That's when she saw how many local businesses wanted to buy food from local farmers, but they didn't know how to make it work. So, H. stepped in. "I feel proud of the fact that I can show how possible things are, even when they're still really complex."

She calls herself "a supply chain facilitator" for farmers. (A supply chain facilitator is the person who moves a product to the customer.)

"I'm like a goofy little translator between everyone to make sure that everyone is on the same page and that we can speak the same language to get something across the finish line."

H.'s mother's family comes from Mexico, near the border with Texas, and she often thinks about her grandmother, Maria Consuelo Nieto, who grew up walking back and forth across the pontoon bridge that connected Ciudad Acuña, Mexico, and Del Rio, Texas, to work. "The name Nieto comes from the branch of her family made up of Hispanos and Indigenous people that inhabited northern New Mexico since the 1500s, until the 1930s when my grandfather came with his family to California."

H. says that her grandmother taught her the value of surviving as a chameleon: tough-skinned yet adaptable to many different worlds. "Today, I am indeed a person of many worlds. I'm between ethnicities, between genders, and in my professional life I've worked in so many corners of the food system, from service jobs to nonprofit to government to corporate startup, always hungry to learn everything I could about the particularities and complexities of every space."

TRAILBLAZER: SHEILA TUPUA-SULU

FOUNDER: Fualelagi Farm

WHERE: Vaitogi, American Samoa

ONE WORD TO DESCRIBE: *devoted*

BEGINS HER DAY: at 4 a.m. every morning before the extreme heat

SPECIAL SAUCE: owns the largest banana plantation in American Samoa!

PRONOUNS: she/her

"I come from a line of strong women," says Sheila Tupua-Sulu from her perch in the shade of a breadfruit tree on the plantation her family has owned for generations.

When you first meet Sheila, you might not guess that she was in the United States Navy as a young woman. Or that she served in the Gulf War in Iraq in the early 1990s. It's all true.

Sheila grew up in California, where her grandmother raised her. She spoke Samoan at home and learned how to garden. Her grandma would give Sheila and her sister little knives and lead them out into the garden to cut weeds and other plants.

In 2009, after the stock market crashed, Sheila felt pulled to return to her family's banana farm in American Samoa, a US territory comprised of seven South Pacific islands (similar to US territories like Puerto Rico, the US Virgin Islands, and Guam). "Land is family," Sheila says.

LAND IS FAMILY

Her father was the last high chief of the village she came from and wanted to continue his path of traditional farming with her husband, who's also a military veteran. Every morning before the sun rises—and it's still cool outside—Sheila, her husband, and her son venture outside in the dark with machetes to prune bananas. She also grows corn, taro plants, and breadfruit.

"If you have soil, then you have gold," Sheila says.

American Samoa imports most of its food to the island, which is packaged and often processed.

Ultra-processed foods are also known as "ready-to-eat" or "ready-to-heat." Some examples are sugary cereal, candy, store-bought baked goods, soft drinks, chicken nuggets, and hot dogs. These foods lack fiber, protein, and vitamins. They're often high in sugar, fat, and salt, and they might contain artificial colors and additives.

Of course, eating these foods sometimes is fine! Yet a constant diet of processed foods has been linked to diseases, such as heart disease, Type 2 diabetes, obesity, gastrointestinal diseases, and depression.

What are examples of "unprocessed" or minimally processed foods? Fresh or frozen fruits and vegetables, beans, lentils, meat, poultry, fish, eggs, milk, plain yogurt, rice, pasta, and more.

Sheila says that packaged, processed foods contribute to the high obesity rates. "People are not eating our local fruit and fresh produce," Sheila says, determined to change this.

KNOW THE TERRITORY

Did you know . . . the United States includes sixteen lands that are not states?

They are called "territories," and one of these places is American Samoa. (The others are Puerto Rico, Guam, US Virgin Islands, and Northern Mariana Islands.) Yes, everyone who lives here is American.

Did you know . . . that American Samoa is located about halfway between Hawaii and New Zealand?

And the people here speak both Samoan and English!

YOUR TURN!

Can you find 5 more facts about one of the US territories?

BIANCA
DATTA, PHD
MANAGER: Scientific Partner at The Good Food Institute
WHERE: San Francisco, California
ONE WORD TO DESCRIBE: explorer
BEGINS HER DAY: watering her garden and walking to Dynamo Donut for coffee
SPECIAL SAUCE: curious about everything, from butterflies to dinosaurs to sushi
INSTAGRAM: @B.Datta
WEBSITE: BiancaDatta.com
PRONOUNS: she/her

"Food is such an incredible space to be in," says Bianca Datta.

It all started with a nonprofit called New Harvest, a place that "first inspired me to consider working in food," said Bianca.

After getting her PhD from MIT in 2021—where Bianca studied "bio-inspired materials," and more—she landed at New Harvest, where Bianca received "a dissertation award," which she describes as money "for people not in the field who want to move into the field."

That's where she learned that "I could apply my materials background towards making more sustainable foods, while also creating joyful human experiences." This award also gave Bianca the freedom to "pivot into food by doing some summer research while applying for jobs and getting to meet lots of other wonderful and like-minded people," she said.

It worked. Bianca landed a job as a Food Scientist at Black Sheep Foods, a company that makes plant-based meats. "One of the challenges for these plant-based meat products is to try and get something that feels like you're cutting up a steak," Bianca says, adding that it's about aligning proteins in the right way. "Most people who traditionally eat meat like the fibrous muscle texture that you get from an animal."

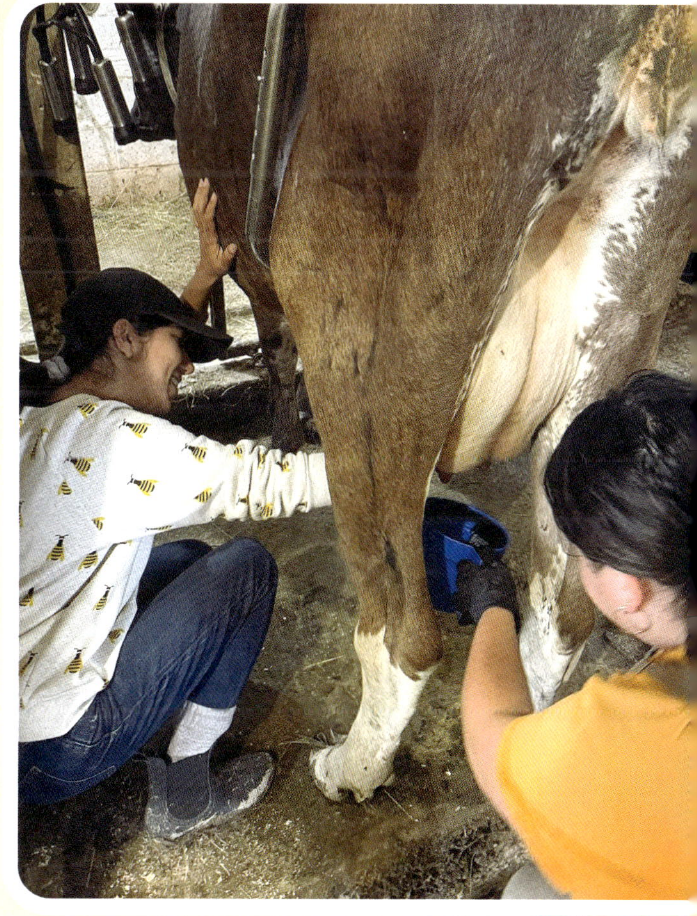

One week, Bianca found herself working on how to make plant-based lamb cut like meat. Then, came duck. And after that, boar. "All of the gamey-tasting meats," she explains.

At the end of most days, she and her co-workers would get together for "sensory panels," which is a fancy way of saying "taste tests."

"Sometimes it's a great experience, and sometimes it's not," laughs Bianca. These days, Black Sheep Foods is selling plant-based "Steak Bites" to restaurants—along with more recent creations like ground lamb and lamb shawarma. (Interestingly, outside of her work, she's *not* vegan.)

As you can probably imagine, Bianca's curiosity runs deep. While in grad school in Boston, she got very excited about "this phenomenon called structural color. I thought it was the coolest thing of all time . . . Most of the colors that we see in the world come from dyes and pigments," Bianca explains. "So my sweater is orange because of the chemicals that we put in it. But some of these organisms in nature are structured in such a way that makes the light bounce around and reflect so we see these really bright colors. Like a peacock's feathers or butterfly wings. It's all very cool—and insane to see happen because these colors are not going to fade over time the way that the chemical dyes do. . . . Structural color can be a tool for more sustainable paints and colorants for things like car paint, textiles, or sensors," explained Bianca.

Because Bianca is such a curious soul—and she wanted to learn more—she decided to sign up to take a farming course in Hudson, New York. She said that this course taught her so much about how to grow food and the roles of animals on farms. "It was also lovely to connect with soil and the earth."

IT WAS ALSO LOVELY TO CONNECT WITH SOIL AND THE EARTH

"I got a much better understanding of the challenges farmers face and the questions they are pondering." This experience inspired Bianca to connect more deeply to the food system through farming, teaching, and volunteering.

Back home, Bianca got a new job at a nonprofit called The Good Food Institute. "I want to focus on scientific collaboration and be more connected to how we grow food," Bianca said. At the end of the day, Bianca is making the global food system better for the planet, people, and animals.

MARÍA INÉS CATALÁN

FOUNDER: Catalán Farm

WHERE: Hollister, California

ONE WORD TO DESCRIBE: *resourceful*

BEGINS HER DAY: getting her youngest child off to school

SPECIAL SAUCE: first Latina farm worker to become a farm owner in the US

INSTAGRAM: @CatalanFamilyFarm

WEBSITE: CatalanFarm.com

PRONOUNS: she/her

"If migrant workers were not here in the United States to work on farms," says María Inés Catalán, "there would be no food on your table."

It's true. When María Inés made the long journey from Guerrero, Mexico, to California, she was twenty-five years old. She was also the single mom of four young children. She knew how to farm, thanks to her grandfather, who'd owned a farm in Mexico where he grew peanuts, corn, cotton, beans, chilies, and sesame seeds.

This was during the 1980s, and María Inés's mother warned her that she might become invisible once she moved to the United States. She'd heard stories about women who came to the US to be farm workers.

María Inés first landed in Salinas Valley, California, where she had some family. She spent her days working diligently, mostly picking broccoli and carrots.

When María Inés was in her thirties, she found out about an organic farming training program that was accepting new students. At first, María Inés laughed at the idea because where she was raised, everyone farms organically—without pesticides. It's how they've farmed for generation after generation, but they don't call it "organic farming."

After graduating from this intensive six-year farming program, María Inés's career took off. Soon, she was selling her produce in more than ten farmers markets around the San Francisco Bay Area, as well as upscale restaurants that knew the best produce came from her farm.

In California, María Inés is known as the first Latina migrant farm worker to own and operate her own certified organic farm. In the United States, she is the first Latina in the country to found a farm that distributes produce through a community-supported agriculture program (also known as a CSA).

She'd never seen kale before moving to California. Today María Inés grows some of the heartiest kale around! María Inés's farm is incredibly diverse and vibrant: She grows strawberries, tomatoes, corn, onions, pumpkins, carrots, and SO many kinds of peppers!

Like many farmers who migrate to the United States, she plants by following the phases of the moon, the way her family always did. She says that the crops grow better this way.

Today María Inés and her family have been running Catalán Family Farms on fifteen acres of rented land in Hollister, California, since 2005. She always dreamed about supporting other immigrant farmworkers to earn a living and own their own land. So in 2021, María Inés founded a non-profit called Pequeños Agricultores en California (PAC), which means "Small Farmers in California." Her goal is to help immigrant farmers acquire organic certification, apply for grants and loans, and work toward owning their own land.

María Inés is also very active in Alianza Nacional de Campesinas (National Alliance of Women Farmworkers), the first national women farmworkers' organization in the United States created by women farmworkers, along with women who are from farmworker families.

According to the United States Department of Agriculture (USDA), approximately half of all farmworkers in the United States, more than one million, are undocumented immigrants.[1]

"An estimated 73% of agriculture workers today were born outside of the United States."[1]

Farmworkers kept food on your table during the pandemic. While most people were told to stay at home during COVID, immigrant field workers were told to keep working.[2]

[1]"Farm Labor," USDA Economic Research Service, accessed December 15, 2024, https://www.ers.usda.gov/topics/farm-economy/farm-labor/.

[2]Miriam Jordan, "Farmworkers, Mostly Undocumented, Become 'Essential' During Pandemic," New York Times, April 2, 2020, https://www.nytimes.com/2020/04/02/us/coronavirus-undocumented-immigrant-farmworkers-agriculture.html.

“I love to be here on the land,” says María Inés. “I’m always laughing when I’m out here. It’s a spiritual freedom here that you can’t imagine. This is my medicine.” María calls her plants “my children.” She said that when her plants are sick, she feels like her children are sick.

She has four grown children, whom she raised on her own. Her son Julio says about his mom: “She’s a very hard worker. She’s always positive.”

When she was forty-nine years old, she adopted a son who’s now twelve years old. “I live for him,” she says. “He’s my love.” María Inés’s younger brother, who transported vegetables, lost his life to COVID-19. “My brother died from coronavirus. He gave his life to provide food for this country. It’s tragic. This was the reality of my people during COVID-19. We were dying to sustain this system.”

María Inés is incredibly generous to her community, donating her produce to schools, churches, and the Homeless Garden Project in Santa Cruz. She set up a farm stand outside the government office in Monterey County on the day when women pick up their WIC (Women, Infant and Children) allowances. In 2022, she donated more than 34,000 pounds of produce to a local food bank!

But in 2023, winter storms flooded María Ines’s home and farm. She lost 70 percent of her crops after water flooded her vegetables. She and her family had to move to a shelter and slowly rebuild. Because María is a woman who has helped so many people, her community knows that now it’s time to support her and help rebuild her farm.

MIGRANT FARM WORKERS

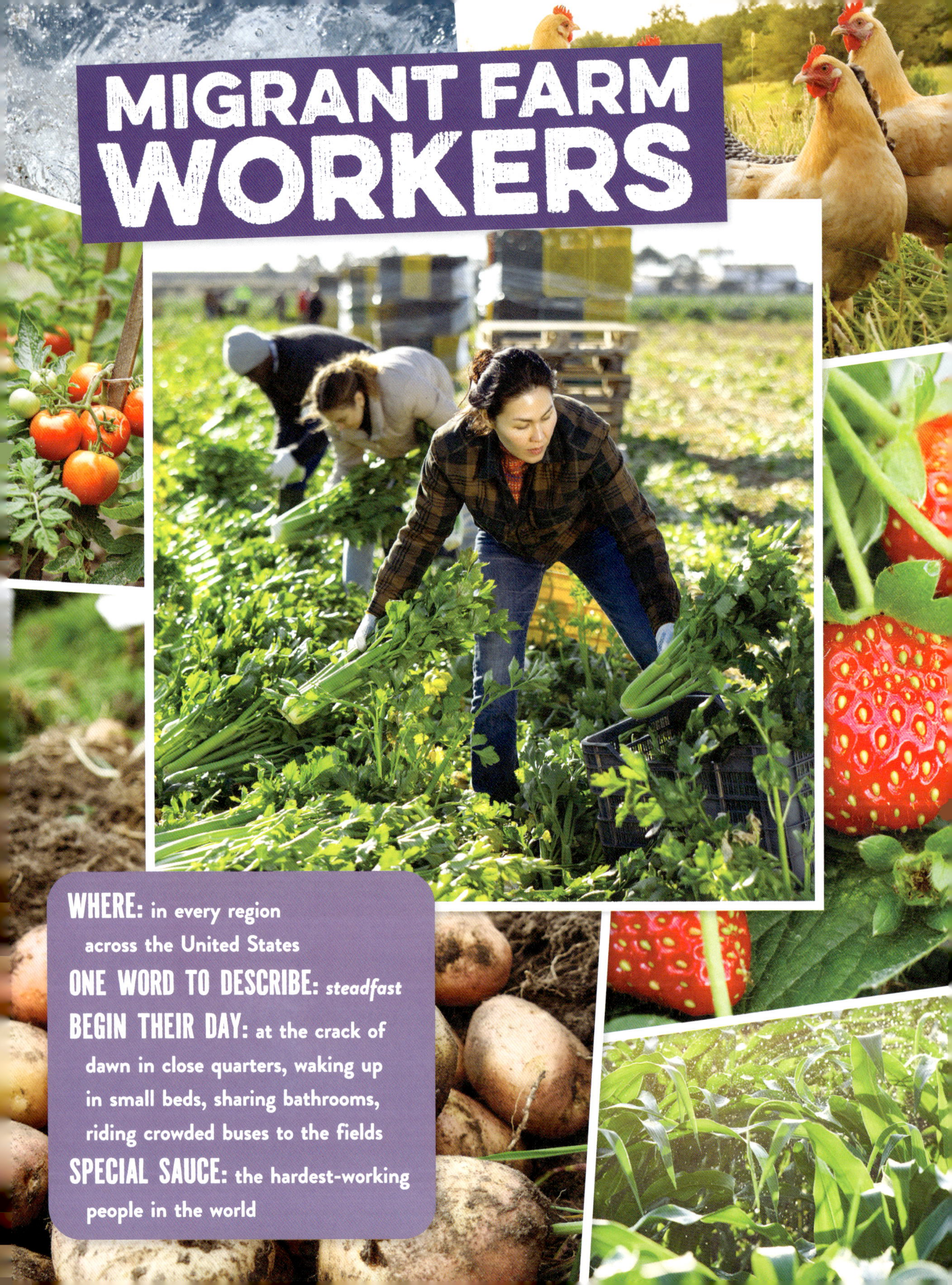

WHERE: in every region across the United States

ONE WORD TO DESCRIBE: *steadfast*

BEGIN THEIR DAY: at the crack of dawn in close quarters, waking up in small beds, sharing bathrooms, riding crowded buses to the fields

SPECIAL SAUCE: the hardest-working people in the world

This chapter is dedicated to the women—and men—who do the longest, most difficult, most underpaid work on farms in the United States to feed people all over the world.

Lupe Gonzalo, for example, was born and raised in a small village in Guatemala. Her home was in the mountains called Loma Linda, which means "lovely hilltop" in Spanish. She has very special memories of growing up here with all of the birds singing in the forest and the river running past her home.

Lupe grew up with eight siblings, and many of her family members were farmers who harvested coffee beans. But her family didn't have a lot of money, and Lupe dreamed of a better life. She'd heard that if you got to the United States, you could be anyone you wanted to be. Lupe wanted to be a teacher or maybe a professional basketball player.

So, as a young woman, Lupe made the long journey to Immokalee, Florida. When she landed here, Lupe found a job as a farmworker in the tomato fields. But the money she earned for working hard all day was barely enough to survive.

Every morning at 4 a.m., Lupe walked out in the dark to the parking lot and asked someone if there was work today on the farm. If the answer was "yes," she got ready, boarded the bus, and waited for hours for the dew to dry on the tomato plants so she could start picking. She was very strong, and she picked fast to fill her bucket.

Lupe worked tirelessly in the hot sun. She filled her bucket over and over again with vegetables. Some days, the farm owners harassed her and the other women by touching them. If women spoke up, the men did not listen. But Lupe knew that if she spoke up, she'd lose her job. And she needed to feed her family.

"We also have rights," Lupe said. "We are human beings, and we deserve respect."

Lupe also wanted to send some money home to her family in Guatemala, but she barely made enough to live. She wanted to go to school. She wanted to play sports with friends after work.

Soon, Lupe became a mother. She'd wake up at 3:30 a.m. every morning to make food for herself and her children. Then, she'd drop her children off at another woman's home so she could get to the fields.

On the field, Lupe did not get paid by the hour. She got paid for each full bucket of tomatoes: fifty cents per bucket. In order to get paid, she needed to fill 100 to 150 buckets per day. If it was scorching hot, taking a break for water might mean not getting paid.

One day while Lupe was working in the field, some people came to visit from an organization called the Coalition of Immokalee Workers, or CIW. The people from CIW told Lupe and the other farmers that they were investigating how farm workers were being treated.

They asked in Spanish:

"HAVE YOU EVER SPENT A DAY WORKING IN THE FIELD BUT NOT GOTTEN PAID?"

"HAVE YOU EVER FELT AFRAID THAT IF YOU SPOKE UP ABOUT, SAY, NEEDING TO DRINK SOME WATER, THAT YOU MIGHT LOSE YOUR JOB?"

Lupe felt relieved to be heard. She started going to CIW meetings to learn more. She wanted to help her fellow farmworkers. At these meetings, Lupe heard about the "Fair Food Program," a strategy that CIW started to get big companies to pay more for fruits and vegetables so farm workers could get fair wages and treatment.

When you go to McDonald's do you think about what it took to get that sliced tomato on your burger? That's what the "Fair Food Program" (or FFP) does: it partners with farm owners, farmworkers, and food companies to increase the price of, say, tomatoes by one cent per pound in order to double every farmworker's paycheck. In the end, this only costs every American family forty-four cents extra per year.

Lupe was inspired. She wanted to do more. So Lupe traveled to Boston, Massachusetts, to march with activists who demanded that big grocery store chains pay more for produce in order to pay farmworkers more. For the first time, Lupe saw the snow. She was in awe!

Today Lupe is on the staff of the Coalition of Immokalee Workers, and she's a recognized leader who stands up for the human rights of workers.

Every February 3rd in the United States, businesses rally together by closing their doors for one day—in order to prove how much immigrants contribute to this country's economy.

The CIW says that Lupe is a woman who "immediately saw an opportunity to right the historic wrongs that plagued US fields, and has never looked back since. Through her more than a decade of work with the CIW, Lupe has become a prominent leader in a global human rights movement centered around the Worker-driven Social Responsibility model, which ensures humane working and living standards for low-wage workers, and which was born in the same Immokalee, FL, fields in which Lupe toiled when she first arrived to the U.S."

AN OPPORTUNITY TO RIGHT THE HISTORIC WRONGS THAT PLAGUED U.S. FIELDS

You probably recognize the names of the stores and restaurants that have ALL joined the Fair Food Program to pay and treat farmworkers fairly, thanks to Lupe and other farmworkers: McDonald's, Walmart, Whole Foods, Trader Joe's, Subway, Chipotle, and KFC.

Young people were a big part of this push to get companies to pay more to farmworkers. For example, in 2005, The Coalition of Immokalee Workers boycotted Taco Bell, which means they asked people to stop buying food from Taco Bell. Students at 22 colleges across the United States stopped buying Taco Bell on their campuses. The chains had trouble operating with fewer customers. After almost four years, Taco Bell agreed to sign a Fair Food Agreement. This means that the company agreed to pay a "penny more per pound" on its tomatoes to be passed on to tomato farm workers. They also agreed to work with The Coalition of Immokalee Workers to improve life in the fields for farmworkers.

However, some big supermarkets—including Kroger and Publix—have refused to join the Fair Food Program. Wendy's fast food restaurant has also declined to join the FFP to pay a fair price for Florida tomatoes.

Today, Lupe hosts a daily radio show on CIW's community FM station. She also has weekly women's group meetings, responds to complaints of abuse in the fields, and supports farmworkers who have not been paid. Lupe has been recognized nationally for her incredible tenacity and strength.

In 2023, at one of the biggest annual agricultural events in the United States, the United States Department of Agriculture's (USDA) Agricultural Outlook Forum, Lupe spoke about the exploitation that farmworkers often face, and how to change this.

It was the first time ever that a farmworker was given the microphone to speak at this significant event.

PROTECTING FARMWORKERS IN HEAT WAVES

As heat waves continue to soar around the United States, many farmworkers have died on the job. In South Florida, for example, farmworkers have had to work every day when the temperature is above 100 degrees.

Farmworker advocates have been pushing for years to pass laws to protect farmworkers from extreme heat. The Coalition of Immokalee Workers and The Fair Food Program's work also includes certifying farms that follow a strict set of workplace safety rules. "In exchange, participating farms are first in line to sell their wares to fourteen big produce buyers that include Walmart, Trader Joe's, Whole Foods, and McDonald's," a Washington Post article states.

"The buyers agree to pay a small premium for produce from farms where workers are protected and blacklist farms that get kicked out of the program. In exchange, they can tout their ethical practices, a selling point with a growing number of consumers worried about who produces their food."

However, leaders in states like Florida continue to block such protections. In 2024, Florida Governor Ron DeSantis signed a law to prevent cities or counties from creating protections for workers who are working in the fields in dangerous, blazing heat. Some of these protections included short breaks to drink water and rest, and provide access to shade. Currently, only four states—California, Washington, Oregon, and Colorado—have heat rules to protect farmworkers.

TRAILBLAZER:
REBECCA SOM CASTELLANO
PROFESSOR: Boise State University
WHERE: Boise, Idaho
ONE WORD TO DESCRIBE: dedicated
BEGINS HER DAY: preparing for her classes
SPECIAL SAUCE: Working hard to shine a light on farmworkers
WEBSITE: https://www.boisestate.edu/sociology/adjunct-faculty/faculty-staff/rebecca-som-castellano/
PRONOUNS: she/her

Rebecca is a sociology professor at Boise State University in Idaho, and for years, she has been concerned about how pesticides are affecting farmworkers. Especially women.

Pesticides are chemicals sprayed on plants to destroy pests and disease. In one study, Rebecca worked with other researchers to collect urine samples from Latine farmworkers in Idaho and study how much exposure they'd had from pesticides on the field.

"Our work really highlights and reaffirms the fact that farmworkers are really invisible, and our food system is built on their labor," Rebecca says.

"THEY WORK HARD JOBS AND LONG DAYS, AND THEY DON'T GET PAID VERY MUCH."

As a sociologist, Rebecca studies and researches human and social dimensions of environmental and agrifood system changes. "Agrifood" means the commercial production of food by farming. In other words, what journey did your food take before it reached your plate? It started with farming and harvesting your food, then transporting it to stores and selling it—everything until you purchased this food to eat.

Rebecca says that many people have this false idea that farmworkers are not skilled. The opposite is true. Every day, it takes tremendous skill and knowledge to work in the fields. "For many farmworkers, this may be the only employment they have access to. So it's meaningful for many of them. Many of them take pride in their work, many of them have a lot of ecological knowledge that we can all benefit from."

Rebecca adds that "one thing we can do to help protect farmworkers from pesticides is inform ourselves about pesticide use in food, and how this impacts those who grow and harvest what we eat." (Most organic produce has not been sprayed with pesticides.)

AMBER BELL

CO-FOUNDER: Sankofa Farms

WHERE: Efland, North Carolina

ONE WORD TO DESCRIBE: *optimistic*

BEGINS HER DAY: mobilizing three young sons for school!

SPECIAL SAUCE: seeing the good in all things is how she vibes

INSTAGRAM: @SankofaFarms

WEBSITE: sankofafarms.com

PRONOUNS: she/her

Every morning, Amber Bell rallies her three boys—ages two, seven, and nine—off to school, then circles back home to study.

Amber is a certified doula, meaning someone who supports a mother before, during, and after the birth of her child. She's studying for an exam to get certified as a lactation consultant to support women with breastfeeding.

"I'm hoping to pass with flying colors," Amber said.

Amber is ready to sign on mothers-to-be as clients to her business, which she is calling Mahogany Joy.

"My favorite word is *joy*," Amber says. "I choose joy because there's always going to be times when life will just get you down. It's about honoring the joy that's already inside of you. You don't have to look elsewhere."

Amber knows this inside and out. She was twenty years old when she and Kamal had their first baby. "In college, I was with Kamal less than a year and we got pregnant," Amber says. "This is full circle because now I'm studying lactation and how to be a doula; I've been tapped into this, and seeing it all now is just so mind-blowing. I just want to be the support that I wish I'd had."

Amber's goal is to connect her work back to the farm in Cedar Grove, North Carolina, a farm that she co-founded with her husband, Kamal. After all, mothers and babies need healthy food to thrive. As Amber reads about maternal health and lactation, the farming crew works outside her window, picking peppers, tomatoes, lettuce, and cucumbers. The sun shines down as they make their way from row to row.

"It's the coolest thing ever to me—these vegetables are made with love and so much hard work." At some point, Amber will venture outside and yell out, "Hey, we are low on kale in here!" Kamal will give her a thumbs-up. "I fuss at Kamal at all the time," she laughs.

"Even if I'm not out there every day, tending to the crops like Kamal is, I'm a farm owner, supporting and raising our children here," Amber says. "It's all very valuable, and my children have so many opportunities here, from picking vegetables to beekeeping. Hopefully, they'll remember this when they're older and keep on passing the torch for generations and our family."

Their kids are also learning how to take care of beehives and chickens. They currently have more than forty beehives. Their seven-year-old son, Akeem, loves the bees so much that his parents run a beekeeping channel for him on Instagram!

Amber and Kamal were both teachers when they decided to buy their plot of farmland, thanks to some financial support from the US Department of Agriculture. They founded Sankofa Farms in North Carolina and are on a mission to create a sustainable food source for families of color in rural and urban areas and to provide new economic and educational opportunities to youth in the community. Sankofa is a West African word that means "remembering your past as you move forward and progress in life."

They both saw how many families struggled to find produce, and when they did find fresh fruits and vegetables, they were expensive. So the couple set out to change this.

"Food deserts are a real thing out here," says Amber. "It's one of the factors affecting our community in a very negative way."

FOOD APARTHEID

Food deserts are areas where there is very little fresh produce available for purchase. Some scholars advocate updating the term to "food apartheid" to more accurately describe the unjust reasons why some areas lack access to fresh food. Think about the following:

- **Where do you and your family shop for food?**
- **How far away is your closest grocery or convenience store?**
- **How long does it take to drive there?**
- **Does your grocery store sell fresh produce?**

For people living under food apartheid, produce options are limited, or they have to travel quite a long distance in order to buy fresh produce.

Kamal and Amber are changing this: They hire local teens to work year-round on their twelve-acre farm. Amber wants young people to feel hopeful. "You don't have to feel like you are less than or lacking. I think we're just a testament of that. . . . Kamal has always been intentional about helping people," Amber adds. "He would say, 'How am I going to help Black people?'"

"Sustainability is about longevity," Kamal explains. "We should be able to pass our farms to the next generation."

It's why he and so many other farm owners are focused on youth. "Young people, for us, is how we address sustainability," says Kamal. "It means having human interactions. It means ensuring that youth look at farming as a potential career."

In the afternoon, Amber will circle back to pick up her sons, offer them healthy snacks, then whisk them off to soccer practice. "Yeah, all boys. It's just, it's very fun, and also stressful at times," Amber laughs.

At the end of the day, Amber simply shows up as her truest self. "I was in a youth group when I was younger, and we were out hiking. At one point, one of our leaders tried to tell us, 'The real you is more attractive than the person you ever try to be.' I felt that deep within me. That's why I've tried to embrace every part of myself and to just be genuine. The world needs more of that."

TRAILBLAZER: UGOADA IKORO

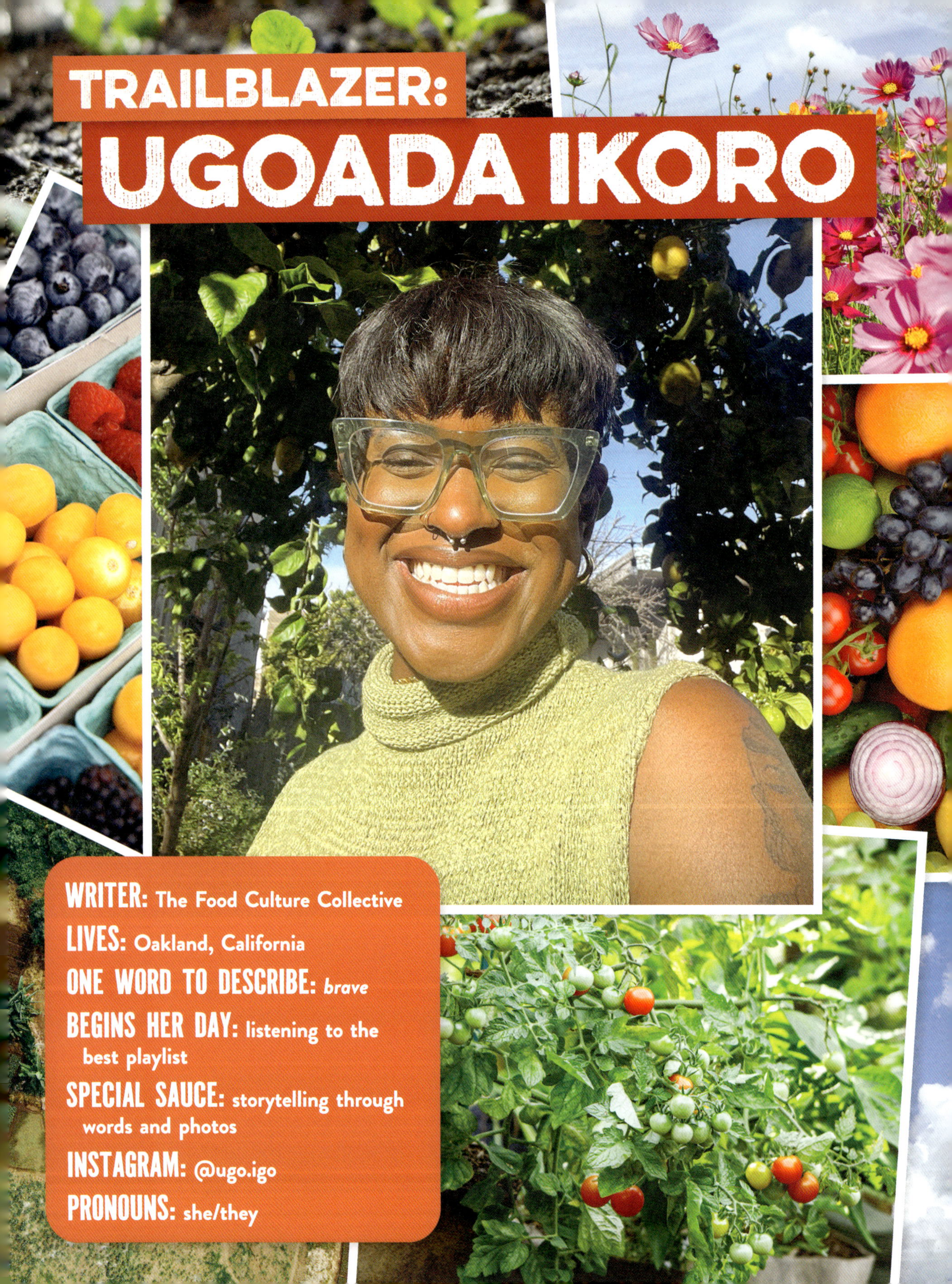

WRITER: The Food Culture Collective

LIVES: Oakland, California

ONE WORD TO DESCRIBE: *brave*

BEGINS HER DAY: listening to the best playlist

SPECIAL SAUCE: storytelling through words and photos

INSTAGRAM: @ugo.igo

PRONOUNS: she/they

Ugoada Ikoro, known as Ugo, grew up in New Jersey with her parents who had emigrated from Nigeria. "I come from a determined line of women who want to make the world a better place," she says.

Her mom studied law in the United States, and every summer, they'd go back to Nigeria to visit family. Ugo felt very close to her aunt, who'd established a foundation to support women, widows, and deaf and visually impaired individuals in the southeast city known as Enugu.

"One of the many things my aunt does is support the only soccer team league for the blind in Nigeria. They've even been able to compete on the world stage multiple times."

Ugo always loved to write, and as she grew up, she began to think about the connections between her home in Africa and Black farmers in the United States. She felt pulled to tell these stories.

"In my mind, it looked like a plant beginning at the base of its root structure unfurling out to the flower," Ugo says. "I started to ask myself about the stories that are grounded in the experiences of Black farmers and sharecroppers, and our ancestors who were forced into slavery. I thought about how we've been creating community through practices rooted in land care amidst the never-ending violence."

On her own, Ugo began to research the stories of Black and Brown farmers in the United States. She'd just moved to Oakland, California, and that's when she applied to be a "Digital Food Culture Fellow" at the Food Culture Collective.

The Food Culture Collective was thrilled to bring Ugo on board to tell and show the stories of "Black Food, Love & Liberation." The stories that follow sprung out of the vibrant historical and contemporary experiences of Black gardeners, farmers, and everyday people who were crafting spaces of liberation and empowerment through the power of food. Ugo recently completed a multimedia digital exhibit, Into the Black Femme Ecoverse, following the lives of four Black femme farmers, inviting us to ask ourselves, "What future do we dream for the future descendants of Mother Earth?"

Ugo spent many afternoons at The African American Museum and Library in Oakland, browsing through old photos and documenting stories about the people and neighborhood where she currently lives. She notes how much has changed in Oakland since the 1960s—and how much has not. "There is one grocery store that is around the corner from me, but when it closes at 7 p.m., there's nowhere else you can go to buy food. The community has done its best to shoulder the burdens of food apartheid."

WHAT FUTURE DO WE DREAM FOR THE FUTURE DESCENDANTS OF MOTHER EARTH?

She feels proud to work with an organization that's rooted in justice and liberation. "We're lifting each other up, through the remembrance of our foodways, to uncover the dreams that are within us."

BLACK FOOD, LOVE, AND LIBERATION

"Each week, Ugo captures stories of joy, beauty, community care, and thriving (beyond surviving) hidden beneath mainstream narratives shaping Black foodways and our relationships to the land," the Food Culture Collective says. Have a look at some of the stories that Ugo has documented about Black farmers and their relationships to the land.

For example, in "Unearthing Liberatory Black Foodways in Oakland, CA," Ugo writes:

"In the warm light of an early spring morning, I look upon weathered raised beds in the backyard garden of my home in the unceded Lisjan territory of West Oakland. These beds were built long before I arrived, and as I prep for spring and summer planting, I'm reflecting on what previous families grew and how they tended to their kin with nourishment from this soil. . . .

"What were Black Oakland residents growing in their backyards during the Jim Crow and Civil Rights eras, and how were they feeding their communities? What did expressions of joy, play, and meal-sharing look like within their families?"

JOANNA LETZ

FOUNDER: Bluma Flower Farm

WHERE: Berkeley, California

ONE WORD TO DESCRIBE: *grit*

BEGINS HER DAY: walking the rooftops and through the flowers, plucking off pests and pulling weeds.

SPECIAL SAUCE: dancer too!

INSTAGRAM: @BlumaFarm

WEBSITE: blumaflowerfarm.com

PRONOUNS: she/her

"You're a woman who's shining light in the world," the National Geographic producer told Joanna Letz after filming her for a TV show about her flower farm in Berkeley, California.

And it's true. Joanna grows the most vibrant, gorgeous flowers on one of the largest rooftop farms on the West Coast in the United States. Chocolate cosmos, dahlias, zinnias, and more!

Bluma Flower Farm extends over fifteen apartment building rooftops! When Joanna tells people that she farms on the roof of a building in downtown Berkeley, people often pause and ask, "Wait, did you say a *roof?*"

She never imagined that one day she'd be farming up here. But when another farmer who'd started what was formerly Top Leaf Farms needed to step away, Joanna stepped in to take over.

THINK ABOUT AN EMPTY ROOFTOP WHERE YOU LIVE, AND EITHER WRITE OR DRAW HOW YOU WOULD TRANSFORM THIS SPACE.

- **What flowers would you grow here?**
- **What kinds of flowers currently grow well in your current climate?**
- **Draw, write, or create what you envision.**

"I get to be a scientist, an artist, a technician when I'm working with plants," Joanna says, acknowledging that it was a huge learning curve at first. "The farm never stops." In her Blundstone shoes, she pauses next to a mass of blooming Zinnias. "Sure, it slows down in the winter, but every day I get to learn so many different things.

Joanna grew up in Berkeley and studied history and human rights with a focus on agriculture at Bard College, followed by an Ecological Apprenticeship at UC Santa Cruz.

"Part of the reason I got into agriculture is because this is the place where we have the capacity to change society," Joanna says.

Her grandfather, a Holocaust survivor, was the person who introduced her to gardening. Her grandparents went into hiding in a neighbor's basement during the Holocaust and had to give up their first daughter to another family to be raised.

"My grandparents did get my aunt back after they came out of hiding," Joanna says. "Although they had to convince the person who took her in—at that point, my aunt didn't want to go, but eventually she did."

Joanna's mother was born in a displaced persons camp in Germany soon after. She said that though he (Joanna's grandfather) had a hard life, when he was in the garden, something lifted for him.

She called her farm Bluma in honor of her family's past: The word means flower in Yiddish. "It's healing to get outside," Joanna says. A rooftop garden like Bluma Flower Farm is incredibly gorgeous, but it's so much more than just pretty looks. Roof gardens can grow food, provide homes to wildlife, control the temperature of a building, and offer a beautiful place to come and hang out.

Joanna grows all of her flowers from organic seeds, and she sells her flowers for big events, like weddings. She also hosts a monthly "Golden Hour Hang" when you show up to pick your own flowers on the rooftop. Sometimes, local high school students volunteer here to help her out. Joanna admits that it's "very difficult to start a farm business—but we need more farmers, especially more farmers who are thinking about how to be resilient in a changing climate."

The United States imports 80 percent of its cut flowers from around the world—from Columbia, Ecuador, Holland, and African countries such as Kenya. Joanna implores people to buy local flowers.

"Local flowers support pollinators, the local economy, increase our relationship to the natural world and the seasonality of plants and what's growing in our region," explains Joanna. "As well as supporting small businesses and farmers like me!"

While Joanna doesn't grow the kind of food we eat, she's creating a habitat for the bees and butterflies that pollinate the gardens in the city as well as food for our spirits. Hummingbirds dart around Joanna in the sunshine as she pulls out her clippers to cut some flowers and then pluck off a snail.

"I like knowing that my flowers are bringing nature and joy into people's lives," she says.

HANDS IN THE SOIL

"I love a person who talks kindly to plants,"

poet Camille Dungy writes in her memoir.

Read a passage from Camille Dungy's book, *Soil: The Story of a Black Mother's Garden*. She writes about the years she spent transforming her manicured lawn that sucked up so much water every week in the suburbs of Fort Collins, Colorado, into a vibrant, colorful garden of plants and flowers where bees and butterflies visit.

ADRIONNA FIKE

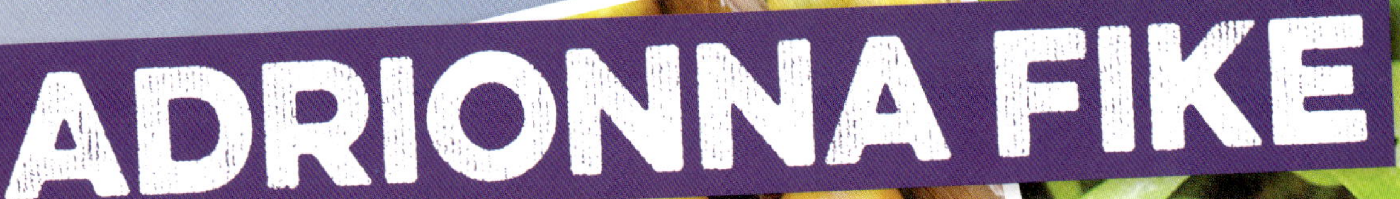

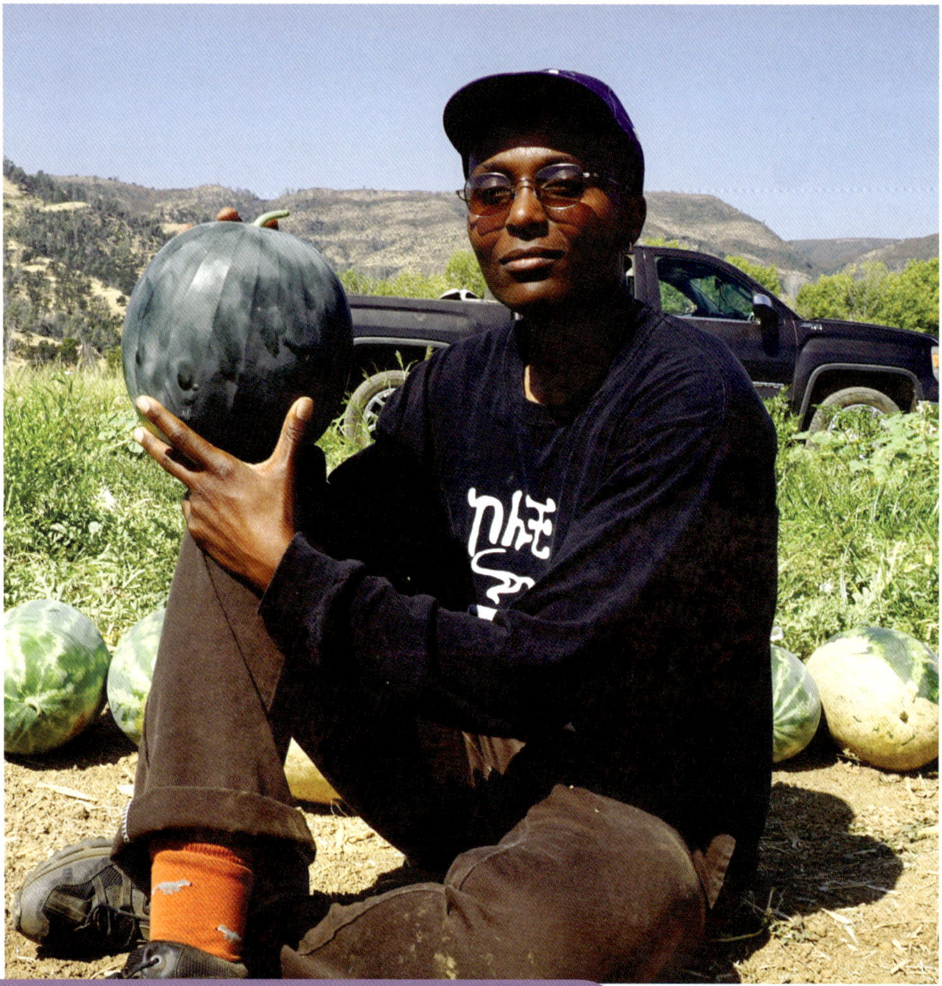

COOPERATIVE ORGANIZER: Cooperation Richmond

WHERE: Richmond, California

ONE WORD TO DESCRIBE: *devotion*

BEGINS HER DAY: listening to jazz

SPECIAL SAUCE: basketball star!

WEBSITE: Visit her outside

PRONOUNS: she/her, they/them, Onna

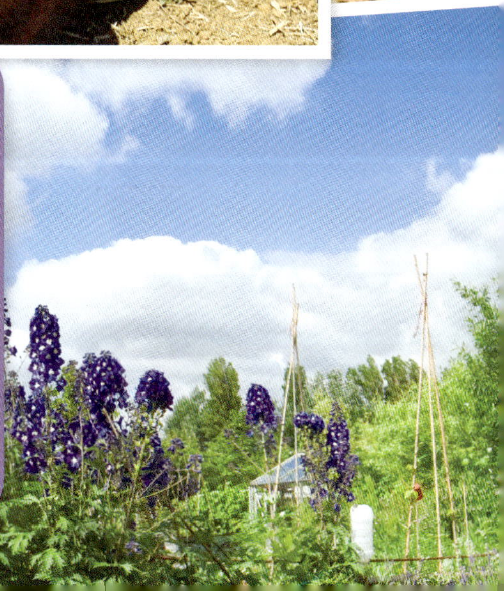

"As a queer black woman, I have a soft spot for middle school students," says Adrionna Fike from Ohlone Land where she lives near Richmond, California. "I was bullied in seventh and eighth grades. A few older kids, struggling to find themselves, would say to me, *Oh, you're gay. Or that's so gay.*"

Adrionna was "still trying to figure it out" about who she was. Being one of the tallest kids at her middle school in the South Bay of Los Angeles didn't make life easier for her.

"Then we all grew up and I saw those same bullies on social media, out, queer, and flaming." Adrionna gently shakes her head. "People take things out on you that they are struggling to see in themselves. They were hurting and struggling back then. I carried that with me for a long time."

In high school, Adrionna found another home in basketball. She felt safe and loved on this team. They won one game after the other and soon became the best high school basketball team in the country! One season, the state of California chose Adrionna—among every single athlete in the state—as the winner of a sportsmanship award, honoring her integrity, community service, and leadership. "I'm really proud of that," she says.

Every player on Adrionna's high school team was offered scholarships to go to college. She had her heart set on Columbia University in New York City. The campus tour also included a visit to Barnard College, the all-women's school that's part of Columbia. When Adrionna walked onto the campus, she knew this was where she wanted to be. She signed up for a class about environmental justice, which means that everyone—regardless of race, color, origin, disability, or income—has the right to the same environmental protections and benefits, as well as meaningful involvement in the policies that shape their communities.

One semester, a class project led her to a garden at a senior center in Harlem. "The seniors wanted to revitalize their garden, so me and two classmates decided to help out and learn about urban gardening among Black elders that semester. We blogged about it for our big class assignment.

"Some of the musicians from the senior center would come out and play jazz in the garden, while our hands were in the soil. Being in that midst was so spiritual. It was the first time I had an experience like that, and I thought, "*Yeah, this is a part of me now*."

Barnard College is also where Adrionna met a woman named Karen Blank, who was the Dean of Studies at Barnard.

"I'd moved across the country to go to school, and Dr. Blank came to all my games," Adrionna says. She would become a woman who supported Adrionna when she most needed it. "As I was going into my sophomore year, I injured myself. It was so severe that I had to stop playing."

Depression set in. Who was Adrionna without basketball? Her grades dropped. Dr. Blank called her into the office. "She said, 'Adrionna, we accept you here to thrive, not to play basketball.' She was so there for me."

ALICE WATERS AND THE EDIBLE SCHOOLYARD

In 1995, a chef and food activist named Alice Waters envisioned what she called an "Edible Schoolyard" at a big, public middle school in Berkeley, California, named Martin Luther King, Jr. It would be the most beautiful, thriving place where children would fall in love with food and learning.

Today The Edible Schoolyard Project continues to flourish on one acre with a garden and kitchen program located at the middle school.

Instagram: @AliceLouiseWaters

After graduating from college, Adrionna moved to the Bay Area of California. She lived a couple of blocks from the Mandela Grocery Cooperative in West Oakland, a worker-owned, Black-owned grocery store that opened more than fifteen years ago.

That's where she met an elder named Dennis Terry. In the 1970s, Dennis volunteered as a young activist to serve free breakfasts to school children, organized by the Black Panthers (see page 34 for more about the Black Panther Free Food Program).

Dennis was one of the original co-founders of Mandela Grocery Co-op. Everyone made an effort to stock the shelves with products from Black farmers and food makers. "I guess he saw my potential and recognized my desire to learn. Dennis Terry oriented me to the depth of cooperatives."

A food cooperative, also called a co-op, is a grocery store owned by its workers and people who live and shop there. Unlike big grocery store chains, food co-ops are independent because the people in the community own the store, not big corporations owned by outside investors.

Dennis used to say that cooperatives "build community instead of abandoning it." Mandela Grocery sells produce from small local farms, along with dairy and meat ranches in the region. When Dennis retired from Mandela Grocery, it opened up a spot for Adrionna to join and be on track to become one of the store's co-owners.

One of Adrionna's goals today is to create cooperative opportunities with people of all ages. Adrionna feels so grateful that she got to learn where food comes from in Harlem and from the stories her mother tells about visiting *her* grandparents' land as a child in Calipatria, California, where they grew watermelons and raised hogs. "In the hot summers, my grandmother would drop my mother and her siblings with my Great-Grandma Mary Jane. They would pick watermelons, bust them on the ground, and eat their hearts out! Every summer, I visit my Black farmer friends in the valley and do the same. Pick watermelons, bust them, and eat their hearts out. It's fresh to be part of this lineage."

From her home on a small farm with her landmates and friends, one of whom is Leah Atwood [see next chapter], Adrionna dreams about "freeing the land." This means, for example, offering literally groundbreaking co-op experiences at local middle schools for students to play, learn, and grow vegetables together. "We need to get the land back into the hands of people who want to learn from the land and grow food. We need to break up the concrete, learn, and rebuild from the soil," she says.

WE NEED TO GET THE LAND BACK INTO THE HANDS OF PEOPLE WHO WANT TO LEARN FROM THE LAND AND GROW FOOD. WE NEED TO BREAK UP THE CONCRETE, LEARN, AND REBUILD FROM THE SOIL.

DECORATE A RECIPE:

Is there a food that is special to you? It could be a food that is part of your cultural heritage. A food that reminds you of a great day or a special person. Or it could just be something delicious! In this activity, you will write out a recipe that is special to you and decorate that recipe to express how it is meaningful to you.

Time: 30 minutes

WRITE:

Think of a dish that is meaningful or special to you?

(If you can't think of one, write down a dish that you want to learn how to make.)

What makes this food special to you? Write down a couple of things that come to mind.

DO:

Find a recipe for the dish or ask a family member for help.

Copy the recipe on a clean sheet of paper.

Decorate the recipe! Try to communicate through your decoration why the recipe is important to you. Don't hold back on the design or colors!

SHARE:

Show your class your recipe and share why it is important to you. If you are doing this without a teacher or class share your recipe with a friend or family member.

Authored by Rachel Mewes

LEAH ATWOOD

CO-FOUNDER: Agroecology Commons
WHERE: El Sobrante, CA
ONE WORD TO DESCRIBE: *dedicated*
BEGINS HER DAY: walking on the farm
SPECIAL SAUCE: a goat whisperer
INSTAGRAM: @aleah_atwood
PRONOUNS: she/they

"Leah is an animal whisperer," says one of her best friends, Adrionna Fike (from the previous chapter) On winter mornings, Leah Atwood pulls on a knitted cap and heads to the goat milking shed to make porridge for them. She's so in tune with the goats that she sometimes senses if someone is in trouble when she's not on the farm.

"Maizey is thirteen years old. She's the great-grandma in the herd, and since she's lost a number of teeth, we soak her grain so it's easy for her to eat. And she gets fed first," Leah says. "Goats like to have clarity and structure. They like to know what to expect. They're more relaxed when they know what the plan is."

The baby in the group is named Dulce. "They know their names," Leah says with a smile. "Goats are such social and curious creatures. They like to be up close to taste and smell. If they are comfortable around you, they usually want to interact! After spending time with them you can see all different personalities: playful, brave, chill, mischievous. And they are totally queer—spend enough time with goats and you'll see a great demonstration of sexuality as a spectrum."

Leah grew up in the redwoods of Northern California, in a small town in Humboldt County. "My dad died when I was five, so my mom pretty much raised my younger sister and me on her own." To make ends meet, her mom took two jobs working as a bookkeeper and as a janitor for a veterinarian. "I don't know how this happened, but my mom ended up helping with a lot of veterinary activities; she was really good with animals."

"Over the years we ended up with a lot of animals people decided they couldn't care for—we had dogs, cats, horses, chickens, and turkeys. My home was a hub of animal activity," Leah says. "One of my favorite things as a kid was to wake up and run out to the chickens to look for the eggs."

When any of their pets ran into trouble, Leah's mom knew what to do. "If one of our dogs got porcupine quills in its face, my mom would give them anesthesia at home and pull out hundreds of quills one by one."

Leah says that she learned how to communicate with animals by watching her mom and pets. "Animals communicate in so many nonverbal ways," she explains. "I think there is so much to learn from our animal relatives on how to listen and communicate in embodied and honest ways."

When Leah was in high school, she set her mind on learning Spanish and visiting a friend from Ecuador who she met when they were an exchange student. She saved up babysitting money to afford the trip. She was in awe of the small gardens in Ecuador where women grew food for their families. Later, in college, Leah would travel to Costa Rica and work on a small farm that sparked her interest in agroecology, which means farming in ways that work more closely with nature, plants, animals, people, and their environment. Agroecology usually limits the use of chemicals to grow food.

Leah soon joined a group of seven women who tended nine goats and two sheep on part of the thirteen-acre community called Wild and Radish on unceded Ohlone land in El Sobrante, twenty minutes from Oakland, California. Their collective is called the Goat Wild Collective and they share the responsibilities of providing food, water, shelter, and safe space to roam for the animals. In return, they share the bounty of milk, meat, fiber, and companionship between themselves and with other families in the community. (Note: Kanchan Dawn Hunter from page 30 lives at Wild and Radish, too!)

"There is a need for more safe and welcoming gathering spaces for people to come together to build trust, enjoy the good times, and weather the hard times," Leah shares.

Blackberries grow wild here—a sweet treat for people and the goats!—and a little creek runs through the edge of the property. There are dreams to plant hundreds more fruit and fodder trees to feed all the living beings and for one day the goats and sheep to graze and rest underneath their canopy.

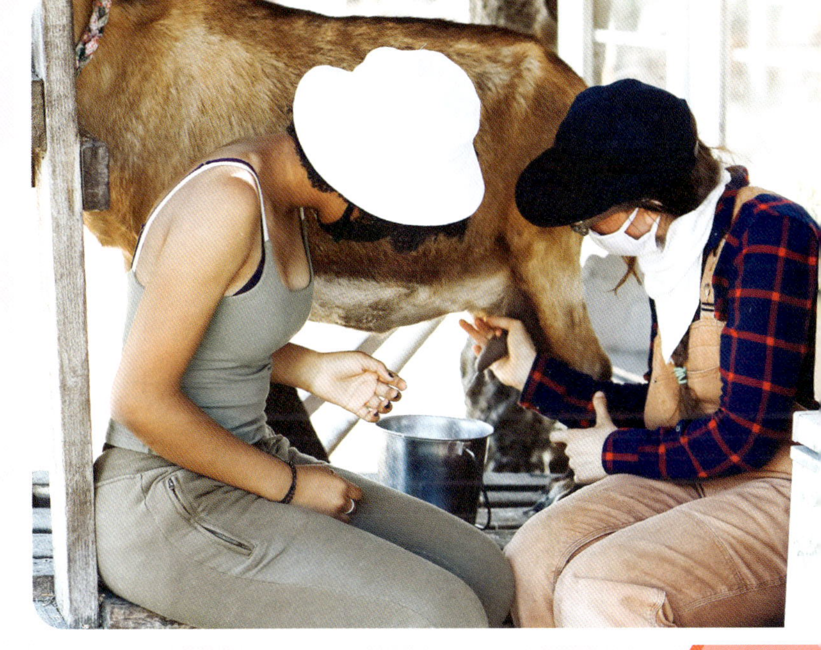

On what Leah calls "harvest and butchering days," members of the collective begin with a morning meditation and gratitude ceremony to honor the goats and give thanks for all their contributions to the land and community. "We feed them their favorite foods, sing them songs, and conduct the whole process on land where the goats are at ease. We try to put ourselves in their place and consider all the elements to minimize fear, stress, and suffering."

During the day, Leah serves as the Partnerships and Resources Steward for Agroecology Commons, a cooperatively run nonprofit that works for regional food sovereignty and collective healing through agroecological land stewardship and farmer-to-farmer education networks. "I am so grateful to collaborate with an incredible team who are whole-heartedly devoted to the land and liberation. Organizing ourselves cooperatively helps us utilize our strengths, shift roles to evolve, and prioritize wellness and not burn out."

IN THE PAST, WE GREW OUR OWN FOOD OR GATHERED IT FROM LOCAL AREAS.

Today, your food often comes from a faraway place in the world.

When we use planes, ships, or trucks to transport fruits and vegetables long distances, farmers must pick them before they are ripe, so they can survive the long trip. This is not only less nutritious and tasty, but it also takes a lot of fuel and causes more pollution.

Let's look at your locally grown produce.

- Are there farms in your state?
- What do they grow?
- What food grows during different seasons?

Take a field trip to visit your local farmers market!

- What foods are being sold here?
- How do the foods sold in your farmers market differ from the ones in your grocery store?
- How do the foods grown in the winter differ from the ones grown in the summer?

Leah also loves to make up recipes, go to the river, and explore trails with her two dog companions, Mahji and Giustino. She signs her emails with the words "Peace and carrots."

In 2018, the Berkeley Food Institute named both Leah and Adrionna "California Food Systems Changemakers." They were profiled in a magazine feature by Berkeley Food Institute called *Hungry for Change*. It featured California's innovators in farming, business, education, and more.

Leah and Adrionna had never met, but they'd heard each other's names in various circles. Fate would put them in the elevator together on the way to a conference in Los Angeles.

"I was in the elevator and I looked up. Adrionna said, 'I know you!'" Years ago, another colleague had given Leah's business card to Adrionna and told her they should connect.

"Adrionna was holding on to my card in her wallet," Leah laughs. "Yeah, we hit it off."

CARING FOR COMMUNITY

During the pandemic, it sometimes felt unsafe to go grocery shopping—especially for older people or those with immune issues. Women farmers in communities all over the world worked together to feed their communities.

Evan Wiig, director of membership and communications at the Community Alliance with Family Farmers (CAFF) in California, witnessed this. Women farmers often lead the charge through some of the worst crises, whether it's recovering from wildfires or sharing tips about how to show up for your community.

"Men say, 'I don't need help, I know everything I need to know,'" Evan says. "But women have the grace to say that 'I can learn a lot.' Maybe this is a stereotype, but maybe it's true."

Evan is also a writer who has interviewed many women farmers who own and run family farms. For example, Evan wrote an essay about how schools are seeking to replace prepackaged vended food with farm-grown produce.

In Sonoma County, California, where Evan lives, he interviewed a woman named Queti Gomez, who works in food services in her school district. Every day, reheated processed food was wrapped in plastic wrap for hundreds of students. "She knew they could do better." So, she set out to replace precooked, packaged meals with locally grown food. She also introduced a new salad bar in the school district, with fresh fruit and vegetables.

DR. GAIL MYERS

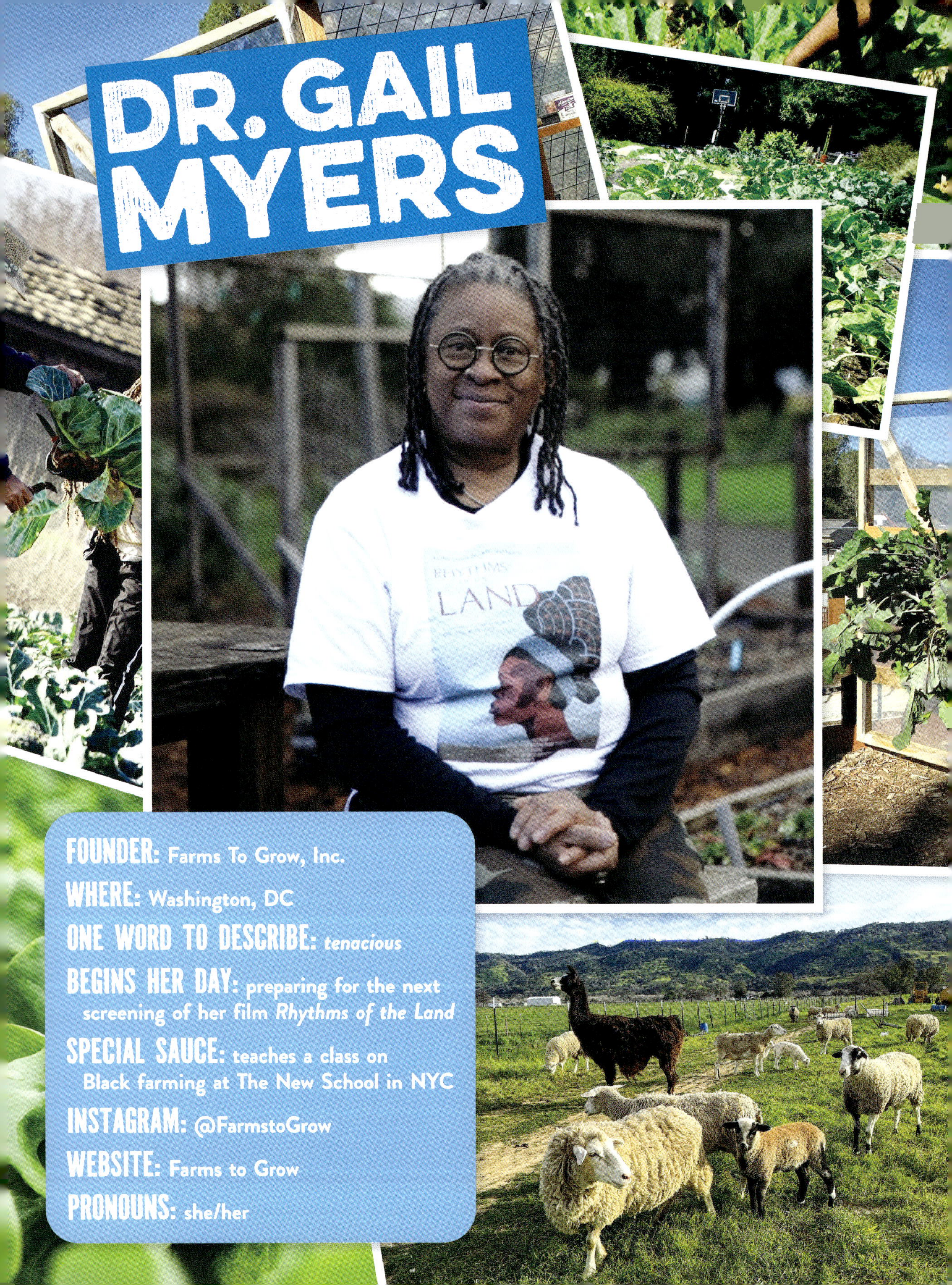

FOUNDER: Farms To Grow, Inc.

WHERE: Washington, DC

ONE WORD TO DESCRIBE: *tenacious*

BEGINS HER DAY: preparing for the next screening of her film *Rhythms of the Land*

SPECIAL SAUCE: teaches a class on Black farming at The New School in NYC

INSTAGRAM: @FarmstoGrow

WEBSITE: Farms to Grow

PRONOUNS: she/her

Dr. Gail Myers adored her Aunt Rose. When Gail would travel to visit her, she'd usually find her out in her garden, weeding. (Aunt Rose gardened all through her nineties and lived to be 104 years old!)

"My Aunt Rose," says Dr. Myers with so much love. "She stands out to me."

Dr. Myers is referring to the film that she spent more than a decade making, a film partly inspired by her Aunt Rose. Gail knew that Aunt Rose would be a part of her dream to make her film, *Rhythms of the Land*, which she titled as such in honor of the rhythms of the farm: the rooster crowing, the geese honking, the cows tromping to the field.

The film honors generations of Black farmers in the southern United States. Dr. Myers traveled all over the South—Texas, Arkansas, South Carolina, North Carolina, Louisiana, Alabama, Mississippi, Georgia, Tennessee, and Florida—to interview more than thirty farmers, sharecroppers, and gardeners.

"Suffice to say, the wisdom and personalities of the elder farmers are infectious," Dr. Myers shares. One of Dr. Myers's goals in making the film was to "connect us to our roots, especially our future farmers and youth."

Gail is a cultural anthropologist, which means someone who studies living societies—what makes them similar to and different from each other. In the field, she researches peoples' cultural, social, biological, and environmental aspects of life in the past and the present.

"I've investigated the history and the legacy of Black farming, starting with the origin of the crops in West Africa and East Africa, and leading to where farming is now," Gail says.

Gail met older Black women and men who shared their stories of farming—many of whom were more than a hundred years old! "I was just in awe of their strength, their love, and their unyielding commitment to their family."

Growing up, Gail would listen to Aunt Rose's stories about being the daughter of a tenant farmer, which means someone who grows crops on land that's owned by someone else. Aunt Rose's parents had to pay rent to a landlord in order to live in their house and farm on their land. White families were almost always the landlords, and Black families were tenant farmers.

Tenant farmers tried to save enough money to pay landowners for the house they lived in and the land they farmed, and to pay sellers for the food they had bought on credit during the year.

The Black farmers who Dr. Myers interviewed for her film were so in tune with the land they planted by the signs of the moon to know if it was time to plant potatoes or corn, and they followed the rhythms of the animals on the land to look for any signs of distress.

Every year, Gail would apply for another grant or fellowship to work on her film. She poured herself into every aspect of filming Black farmers' stories and knowledge for this documentary. She spent more than two decades (yes, that's twenty years!) interviewing Black farmers around the United States to document their losses, struggles, and successes. She spoke to every kind of farmer out there: hog ranchers, dairy ranchers, shrimp farmers, and vegetable farmers.

For example, DeBorah William, the daughter of a Georgia sharecropper, co-founded The Mother Clyde Memorial West End Garden in Atlanta in 1995. DeBorah took over a vacant lot that was covered in trash and turned it into an abundant farm where people in the neighborhood drop by to pick fruits and vegetables. She and others describe "sharecropping" as "share the work, share the crop!"

When she was not teaching or making her film, Dr. Myers became a devoted advocate for Black farmers in the San Francisco Bay Area. So, in 2004, she started Farms To Grow, a non-profit that advocates and supports Black farmers.

Farms To Grow, Inc. supports underserved farmers to keep their farm operations and establish farming as a viable career for future generations. Underserved farmers may include Native Americans, Hispanics, other minority groups, women, the physically challenged, and limited access organic farmers. Several years later, she started the Freedom Farmers Market in Oakland to provide a market for Black farmers who couldn't get a space at white-dominated farmers markets.

When Dr. Myers was managing farmers markets, she noticed that none of the farmers were Black. "We had created a space that was unapologetically Black. And it was positive around food."

"I remember one day, this Black man came to the Farmers Market in Oakland, and we started talking. He told me, 'This is one of the safest places I've been in a long time. Yeah, I feel safe here.'"

Dr. Myers adds that "we need more places like this . . . with Black people, Black music, Black farmers."

Dr. Myers says that Black farmers are the foundation of farming in the United States—and she's determined to bring them to the forefront and ensure they are paid their worth. She co-founded The Farmers XChange platform, which was originally organized and developed by three African American women who had a vision to see farmers remain financially viable by directly interacting with consumers, other farmers, farm affiliates, hotels, restaurants, and grocery stores.

Today Dr. Myers lives in Washington, DC, and often travels around the country to share knowledge about the legacy of Black farmers.

ELIZABETH COUSE

FOUNDER: Liberation Permaculture

WHERE: Puerto Viejo, Costa Rica

ONE WORD TO DESCRIBE: *authentic*

BEGINS HER DAY: a morning walk on the beach with her dog

SPECIAL SAUCE: landing halfway around the world and creating a community

INSTAGRAM: @ElizabethCouse and @liberationagriculture

PRONOUNS: she/her

If you're wondering how Elizabeth Couse got from upstate New York to Costa Rica, she will begin by telling you that she was born in China. When she was one year old, her mom—a single mom—adopted her and brought her back to the United States.

"Shortly after I was adopted, she was tragically diagnosed with terminal cancer and passed away when I was six," Elizabeth says. "I went to live with my mom's sister and brother-in-law, whom I would consider my mom and dad growing up."

She describes her family as "Irish Catholic" in a "predominantly affluent white neighborhood." When Elizabeth was in third grade, other kids started to comment about her Asian identity. "Mom had to explain to me how I was adopted, that I was Chinese, and that I was kind of different from the other kids."

When she was thirteen years old, her mom—whom she refers to as "my third mom"—passed away, followed by her dad when she was in her early twenties. Elizabeth shares this story to communicate how much she desired and yearned for "a sense of belonging that I never really had either from my family or just from the culture and my community in America."

The older Elizabeth got, the more she saw she wasn't alone in her feelings. She also says that to fill that void, people turned to superficial things, like buying new clothes. She did the same as a teenager, and she realized that brand names or social media still didn't give her a true sense of belonging.

Elizabeth went to Cornell University and earned a degree in International Agriculture and Rural Development with minors in Community Food Systems and Communications.

"My first semester, I took a class called Intro to Sustainable Agriculture," Elizabeth says. "We met once a week for four hours in the afternoon to visit different farms or nonprofit food projects going on. I fell in love with it; it was my favorite. I loved learning what intersectional agriculture is." Intersect means that two or more issues or ideas cross. So, intersectional agriculture means that growing food crosses with another concept, such as race, gender, disability, sexuality, or another concept.

"I'VE ALWAYS CARED SO MUCH ABOUT PEOPLE AND ALL THE PROBLEMS IN THE WORLD, LIKE CLEAN WATER OR WOMEN'S RIGHTS OR SUSTAINABILITY—FOOD'S SOMETHING THAT REALLY LINKS SO MANY DIFFERENT ISSUES TOGETHER. . . . IF WE CAN CHANGE THE FOOD SYSTEM, WE CAN CHANGE SO MANY FACETS OF SOCIETY IN OUR WORLD. . . . FOOD AFFECTS EVERYTHING."

After graduating from college, she made a very brave decision: to leave the United States and move abroad to a small town on the Caribbean coast of Costa Rica.

"It's commonly cited that rural smallholder farmers produce 70 percent of the world's food, and over half of rural smallholder farmers are women," says Elizabeth. "That would mean that somewhere between 35 percent and 40 percent of the world's food comes from women smallholder farmers compared to 30 percent from industrial agriculture. This means that women smallholder farmers grow more of the world's food than industrial ag[riculture] does."

Elizabeth's mission to community farming has stayed clear. "I founded a movement called Liberation Agriculture to commit to justice and liberation in the food system. . . . I advocate for a diverse sustainable agriculture movement—anyone can be a part of it and really honors Indigenous leaders as the leaders of the movement."

Now in her late twenties, Elizabeth has taught permaculture courses, led sustainability retreats, and even opened a "farm-to-table vegan restaurant" in town.

"I'm most proud of creating a sense of community and stability around me. I'm very grateful for my Costa Rican friends and colleagues," says Elizabeth. "The community here is amazing. And obviously, I've done a lot of intentional, conscious things to create that around myself—I don't necessarily have that inherently just from family."

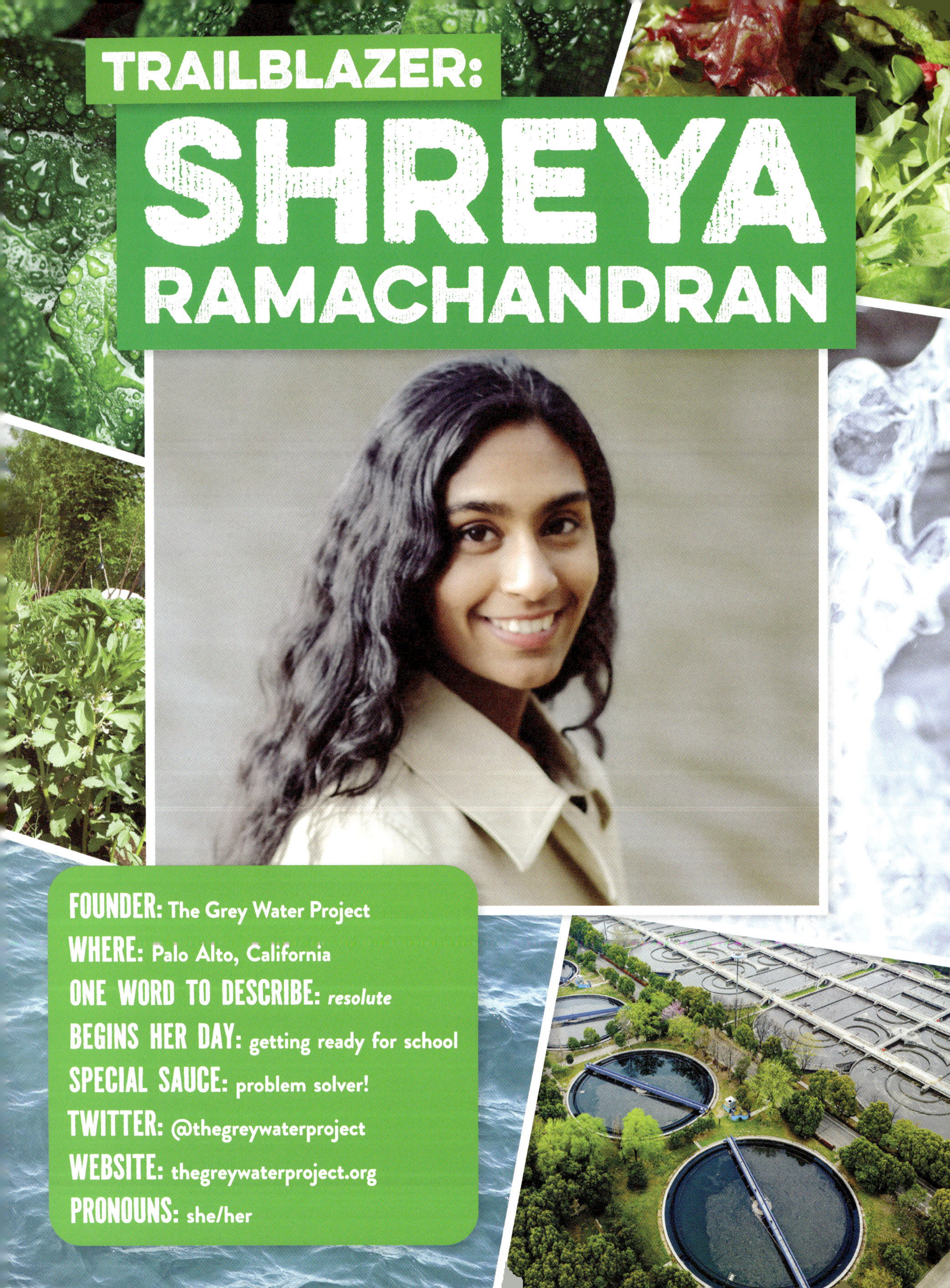

TRAILBLAZER: SHREYA RAMACHANDRAN

FOUNDER: The Grey Water Project
WHERE: Palo Alto, California
ONE WORD TO DESCRIBE: *resolute*
BEGINS HER DAY: getting ready for school
SPECIAL SAUCE: problem solver!
TWITTER: @thegreywaterproject
WEBSITE: thegreywaterproject.org
PRONOUNS: she/her

Shreya Ramachandran was only 12 years old when she first started researching grey water.

Shreya is a student at Stanford University. As a teenager, she founded a nonprofit called The Grey Water Project to promote the reuse of grey water. Grey water reuse is a process that recycles water.

White water—clean drinking water—becomes grey or black water when we use it! Grey water is the water from sinks, showers/baths, and laundry. Black water is water used for toilet flushing and in kitchen sinks. Any "used" white water is water lost to leaks.

In other words, grey water is water that you've used *once* in your home—and can be used again for some other purpose to conserve how much water you use. But it is *not* for drinking!

"You can use grey water to water, or irrigate, your plants," Shreya says.

HOW CAN YOU SAVE WATER?

In your own home, there are many ways to save and reuse water. For example, keep a bucket in your shower/bathtub. Every time you run the water to heat it up, the bucket will fill up—and you can use this water to nourish your plants every day!

Set up buckets to catch and store rainwater to water your garden.

Install a laundry-to-lawn system, which allows you to reuse the water from the laundry rinse cycle to water trees and plants!

TRACKING YOUR WATER USAGE

Shreya created The Grey Water Curriculum when she was in high school! She shows how communities can recycle and reuse water.

The first step to learning how you can conserve water is taking a closer look at how you use it! Take note of how you are using water as you go about your day:

How long are your showers, how many times a week do you do laundry?

Time the activities (e.g., showers), or count the number of times they are done (e.g., laundry) and calculate the flow rate.

Where is the most water being used?

ANA ELISA PÉREZ QUINTERO

FOUNDER: La Colmena Cimarrona

WHERE: Luján, Vieques, Puerto Rico

ONE WORD TO DESCRIBE: *tireless*

BEGINS HER DAY: Out in the field, working the land

SPECIAL SAUCE: accomplished beekeeper

WEBSITE: colmenacimarrona.org

PRONOUNS: she/her

When Ana Elisa Pérez Quintero was thirteen years old in middle school in Puerto Rico, she knew exactly what she wanted to do when she grew up: take care of the ecosystem for her community.

She had heard that some hotel developers were planning to build resorts on the most beautiful, precious nature reserve on the coast of Puerto Rico. It's called the Northeastern Ecological Corridor, and it is where enormous leatherback sea turtles nest.

These turtles are endangered, and they swim thousands of miles to get to this beach; it's one of the most important nesting areas for leatherback sea turtles in the Caribbean. Also, more than nine hundred species of plants and animals live in and around the coast here! When Ana Elisa found out that these developers were going to build 3,500 hotel rooms, numerous golf courses, a shopping mall, and more, she knew this would destroy the forests, lagoons, and beaches here.

She joined a movement to protect this land. For many years, Ana Elisa and her community rose up against the construction of the two mega hotel resorts. Ana Elisa was the activist who went to schools to speak to young people about what was happening and to encourage them to speak up too. She founded a group called GAIA (Grupos Ambientales Interdisciplinarios Aliados) in classrooms to lead kids in ecology, art, culture, and environmental activism. Ana Elisa also started three urban gardens where kids could grow food.

When she was twenty years old, she won the prestigious Brower Youth Award for all of the work she did to protect Puerto Rico's coast. (The Brower Youth Awards recognizes the work of six young leaders who are making strides in the environmental movement.) Thanks to the tireless persistence of the Puerto Rican community, Ana Elisa was able to keep the developers at bay. Today activists are trying to help the government purchase the land in the corridor to protect the land here.

Ana Elisa's interest in community health continued throughout her life, sparking the making of new community gardens and facilitating agroecology courses in multiple communities in Vieques—an island located about seven miles off the east coast of Puerto Rico—and the Caribbean. She participated in a farmer-to-farmer exchange in Vieques that led to the creation of La Colmena Cimarrona, an organization she co-founded, dedicated to achieving food sovereignty for the island and archipelago. After Hurricane María, it became even more obvious how important growing food in Vieques was; food shortages are a normal thing on the island, but the lack of maritime transportation sparked a crisis. The farmers and community organized workshops, community kitchens, and more through the organization that is now La Colmena Cimarrona.

"Ana Elisa runs the educational farm within the organization. One of La Colmena's projects is La Colectiva Agrícola Viequense, a farmers network of mutual support. Due to Vieque's history of colonization, only six farms exist on the island, the biggest one being the one run by La Colmena. They are working to train more youth and folks to learn how to farm.

If you visit Ana Elisa, the first thing she might ask is if you're allergic to bees. Because in addition to growing bananas, avocados, and tomatoes (and so much more!), she's an expert on beekeeping and has many hives on her farm.

Most likely, Ana Elisa will also share why she named her farm La Colmena Cimarrona. La Colmena Cimarrona translates roughly to "The Maroon Beehive." In 1943, the United States Navy arrived on the island of Vieques, claiming that this land belonged to them. Puerto Rican families, however, had lived here for years, farming and raising families. According to the people of Vieques, the US military cut off the water to their homes and lit one house on fire. The parents of this house told their children to get the beehives from the field and release the bees. Swarms of bees began attacking the US marshals, stinging them. This was one of the creative strategies the Viequenses used to kick the Navy out in 2003 after massive local mobilizations and international support helped end sixty years of occupation.

"Maroons were the slaves that freed themselves from slavery; we believe food is freedom, it is sovereignty, *autodeterminación*. That's why Ana Elisa calls this farm the Maroon Beehive: to honor her community's resistance and struggle for independence. Moreover, because queen bees are the leaders of their colonies, and her farming community is mostly women—the name is a perfect fit!

WOMEN FARMERS RISING UP IN THE CARIBBEAN

There are many women farmers in the Caribbean who are feeding their communities, such as Helen's Daughters in St. Kitts.

Founded by Keithlin Caroo, Helen's Daughters's mission is to amplify women in agriculture through tourism. After working for the United Nations, Keithlin returned home to found a nonprofit to provide training, mentorship, and more for rural women farmers on the island—something she knows that her own mother and grandmother would have benefited from.

If you're visiting St. Kitts, you can see a tour called In the Eyes of a FarmHER to visit a local farm, plant your own seedlings, and make local spices and jams. Keithlin dreams about transitioning her family's farm to run on a hundred percent renewable energy in the near future.

LESLIE WISER

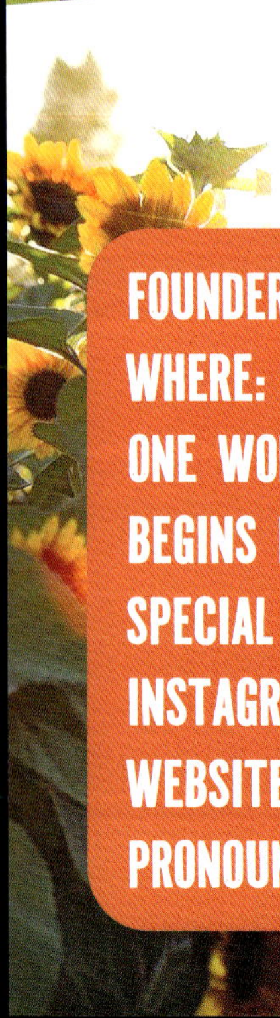

FOUNDER: Radical Family Farms

WHERE: Sebastopol, California

ONE WORD TO DESCRIBE: *determined*

BEGINS HER DAY: getting her two kids to school

SPECIAL SAUCE: growing Asian heritage vegetables

INSTAGRAM: @RadicalFamilyFarms

WEBSITE: www.radicalfamilyfarms.com/

PRONOUNS: she/her

Leslie Wiser strolls down a row of soil to survey her bitter melon seedlings, with of course, her fourteen-year-old dog, Big Bear (also known as Cici), who shadows her close behind. Fourteen years ago, Leslie's spouse was driving on a highway in the Appalachian Mountains of Tennessee when she spotted a little ball of fur alongside the road. She pulled over and scooped up the puppy, who's now a full-grown bear of a dog, and brought her back to Leslie.

"Her favorite thing is gopher patrol," Leslie says about Cici. "Now she is spending more time resting inside by the fire," Leslie says. "She's hard of hearing and we are communicating more with hand signals. She picked them up quickly!"

Even Cici knows that you need to learn fast on the farm. Bitter melon is "one of our most beloved crops," Leslie says. It grows on a vine and is related to zucchini, squash, and cucumber; it's also essential to many Asian meals.

Leslie founded Radical Family Farms out of a desire to connect to her Asian American heritage. Her mom grew up in Taiwan after leaving China during the Chinese Communist Revolution. Her dad's side of the family is German and Polish-Jewish. Leslie didn't start farming until her forties—she brought her kids to the farm as a single mom and literally put her hands in the soil.

Women in California today represent 37 percent of all the producers in the state, according to the most recent USDA Census of Agriculture—which only began tracking these numbers in 2017.

Leslie describes her three-acre farm as "dreamy but so expensive."

"I wanted to use this farm as a way to reconnect with the Asian side of our ethnicities. So, that's what we're doing—we're growing a lot of Korean crops, a lot of Chinese and Taiwanese crops, and then also Japanese, and some Southeast Asian crops as well," Leslie says.

Her favorite vegetables to grow? Chinese Mustard Greens, Long Beans, every kind of basil . . . especially "holy basil!"

FARMERS IN CALIFORNIA GROW SPECIALTY CROPS

Specialty crops are the fruits, vegetables, and nuts that only grow in California—and nowhere else in the United States. Some examples are almonds, artichokes, and broccoli. More than a quarter of the food produced in the US, including most of the country's fruits and vegetables, comes from California, according to the Food & Environment Reporting Network. Thanks to California's long hot summers and mild winters, farmers can keep growing throughout the year.

When the pandemic hit the world, many older people were stuck indoors. It wasn't safe for them to go grocery shopping. Leslie had to do something. She raised money through a grant and private donations to start delivering her vegetables free to older Asian Americans in Oakland, California. Not only were these vegetables familiar to them—and nourishing—but the deliveries also kept them safe.

"A lot of this was driven by the attacks on our Asian elders during the pandemic," Leslie adds. "It's still happening, with seniors afraid to walk on the streets without being pushed down."

Her long-term goal is to dedicate one-third of the produce from her farm to Asian seniors residing in the San Francisco Chinatown's Single Room Occupancy (SRO) buildings through private, tax-deductible donations. "It is part of my cultural heritage to honor our elders," Leslie says, adding that her grandparents on both sides took care of her growing up, so delivering "culturally relevant produce" to Asian seniors is meaningful. "Instead of getting bags of potatoes, they can get Chinese vegetables, produce, and herbs that are familiar to them."

FACING WILDFIRES AND DROUGHTS AS A FARMER

Small farmers like Leslie Wiser face many challenges due to climate change. "There are a lot of environmental disasters on my farm, between the drought and wildfires," she says. "It's really difficult to live here."

Rosie Kaperonis at Azolla Farm in Pleasant Grove, California, is another farmer who has faced her share of fires and floods.

During the 2018 Camp Fire in Paradise, northern California, temperatures rose to more than 106 degrees some days. It wasn't just the heat affecting farmers and the crops, it was the smoke, which left powdery mildew on the crops.

"It's intense to work out in the field," says Rosie, who runs the farm with her partner Scrivner Hoppe-Glosser. "Just the headaches alone. It was hard to breathe. We were wearing respiratory masks in the field, pushing through." When so many people lost their homes in the Camp Fire, Azolla Farm donated produce to World Central Kitchen, a non-profit that helps people displaced by disasters.

In 2023, Azolla Farm flooded in the winter storms. Their crops were underwater for twenty days. They lost more than $35,000 between produce lost and repairs needed.

Note: Azolla is a tiny fern that grows locally on the surface of slow-moving water. It's also called mosquito fern, duckweed fern, or fairy moss. Though small, it's an essential nutrient to other organisms.

KATIE WILLIS

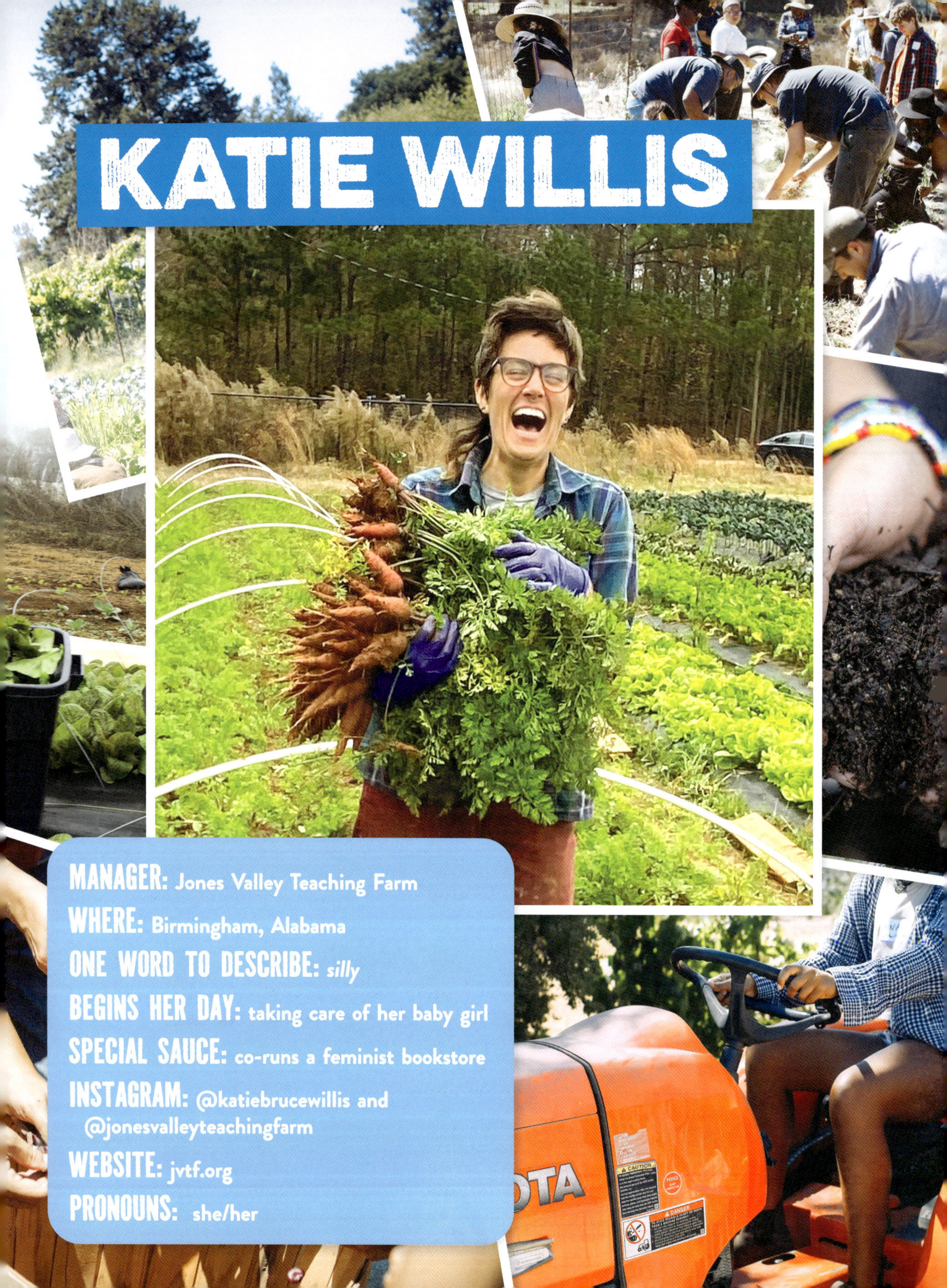

MANAGER: Jones Valley Teaching Farm

WHERE: Birmingham, Alabama

ONE WORD TO DESCRIBE: *silly*

BEGINS HER DAY: taking care of her baby girl

SPECIAL SAUCE: co-runs a feminist bookstore

INSTAGRAM: @katiebrucewillis and @jonesvalleyteachingfarm

WEBSITE: jvtf.org

PRONOUNS: she/her

Katie Willis's shoes are wet after walking in from the field. But she's all smiles. Katie is a grown-up now—and the mama of a nine-month-old baby!—yet here she is, right back on the *same* farm where she worked during high school.

"I hated being in Alabama," Katie says. She knew from a young age that she was queer, and living in the South wasn't easy. Katie describes queer as "not fitting into a specific box or defined gender—feeling very much the fluidity of gender and feeling confined by having my gender put into a box."

In high school, Katie heard about an agri-science class at Jones Valley Teaching Farm. Katie skimmed the questions on the form:

- **Are you good at math and science?**
- **Do you love animals?**
- **Are you interested in the environment?**
- **Are you good at problem-solving?**

Yes, yes, yes, and yes!

"This changed the trajectory of my life and gave me meaning when I didn't feel like I had much," Katie says about the time she spent on Jones Valley Teaching Farm.

"I had a lot of body issues as a high schooler," Katie explains. "Farming allowed me to see myself as a strong person. It reconnected me to my body."

Also, Katie loved the feeling of getting her hands into the soil. "Women can do manual labor and be strong," she says. "Women can be dirty."

"Women are now, like, dominating organic agriculture in this country, as small farmers," Katie adds. "But I think we still have this image of men as if they're out there in the fields doing all that manual labor."

If she could go back and speak to teenage Katie, she'd tell her: "Your body is amazing and perfect the way it is. Your body can do so many things."

When Katie got accepted to Middlebury College in Vermont, she was thrilled. She decided to major in women and gender studies. She wrote a long nonfiction piece called, "Letting It All Go Straight to My Hips: A Journey of the Body," about heteronormative bodies, which won Best Thesis.

"THERE'S A SEXUAL-HARASSMENT EPIDEMIC ON AMERICA'S FARMS"

That's a headline from The Atlantic magazine.

Katie Willis also talks about the sexism she has witnessed—and experienced—during her years farming in different regions.

Sexual harassment means unwelcome sexual advances, either verbal or physical, especially by someone with power or authority. Sexual harassment includes things like joking about someone's sexual orientation or making sexual jokes, comments, or gestures; spreading sexual rumors (in person, by text, or social media); or posting sexual comments, pictures, or videos.

In 2024, the California-based raisin and dried fruit company, Sunshine, agreed to pay $2 million to settle a lawsuit claiming that the company allowed female farm workers to be sexually harassed. The lawsuit accused Sunshine of ignoring complaints and also firing workers when they spoke up about being harassed. Many of the farmworkers only spoke Spanish. Hopefully, this case will make it easier for women to report harassment without fear.

After graduating from college, the last place Katie thought she'd land was back at Jones Valley Teaching Farm. But she loves this land and now appreciates it. "Alabama is one of the most biodiverse states in the country!" Katie says. "That gives me a lot of pride for this state. We have so many salamanders and rare plants that can't be found anywhere else."

Also, after working a variety of different jobs, such as working in a lab to collect data, Katie says, "I don't know how to *not* work with my body."

Today Katie and her partner dream about buying land in Alabama in the near future. She wants to start a native plant nursery, which means a place that sells plants that are native to her region.

When Katie isn't farming, she co-runs a feminist bookstore in Birmingham called Burdock Book Collective. It also runs a "Books to Prisons Project" to match people in prison with pen pals on the outside and get books into prisoners' hands.

Katie's daughter just started eating solid foods, and the other day, she "shoved a whole broccoli floret into her mouth! It was pretty special to see because I'd grown that broccoli. I also made her sweet potato biscuits last week that were from sweet potatoes we'd grown. Growing food that I can also eat and share with my family is really meaningful and makes the mealtimes special."

GROWING FOOD THAT I CAN ALSO EAT AND SHARE WITH MY FAMILY IS REALLY MEANINGFUL.

REWRITING THE NARRATIVE

Caitlin Joseph's job title is a mouthful, but it's a very significant one: Women for the Land Deputy Director at American Farmland Trust. Since 2009, Caitlin says, women have been surpassing men in agricultural education.

More and more women today are also majoring in STEM (science, technology, engineering, and mathematics) to work in science—and, yes, agriculture.

So why aren't women farmers paid as much as men?

Every day, Caitlin works hard to ensure that women-led farms in the United States are profitable, which means they earn enough money to thrive and survive. Caitlin says there are many reasons that farms owned by women struggle financially. "Women leading their own farms also tend to be newer to agriculture," she says, explaining that often men have worked in farming for much longer and therefore already have connections and resources.

Also, many women-led farms are smaller than traditional large-scale operations, so the government hasn't recognized them—and Caitlin thinks this needs to change. She adds that for women-led farms to grow and thrive, farmers need better access to affordable childcare and healthcare, which are often limited in rural areas.

"We need to rewrite the dominant narrative about what a successful, competent farmer looks like," Caitlin says, explaining that women, too, "can drive a combine, run cattle, or raise hogs."

Note: A combine is a machine that harvests crops.

LAYEL CAMARGO

CO-FOUNDER: Shelterwood Collective

WHERE: Cazadero, California

ONE WORD TO DESCRIBE: *passionate*

BEGINS THEIR DAY: with meetings in the middle of the forest

SPECIAL SAUCE: the ability to heal

INSTAGRAM: @shelterwood_collective

WEBSITE: shelterwoodcollective.org

PRONOUNS: they/them

"After all of the rejection I've experienced my whole life as a queer person, I thought, 'This can't happen anymore,'" says Layel Camargo.

That's one of the many reasons Layel dreamed of creating a safe, nurturing place where anyone could show up and feel loved. They envisioned somewhere in nature, where you could grow food in the garden, cook, share meals, laugh, create art under the stars, and heal. Layel has carried this vision for many years—and has not let go.

After graduating from UC Santa Cruz, Layel started working as an Ecological Arts and Culture Manager. They proudly identify as part of the Yaqui tribe and Mayo tribes of the Sonoran Desert, as transgender and non-binary. Layel told their friends about their dream: "I want to buy two acres of land someday." (Close to the same size as, say, a soccer field.)

"I WANT IT TO BE A SAFE, CREATIVE SPACE WHERE ANYONE IS WELCOME."

One summer, Layel traveled to Soul Fire Farm (founded by Leah Penniman in this book) in upstate New York to attend a farming workshop with other people from around the world. Little did they know how this experience would change their life.

Nikola Alexandre, a Black queer forester who'd recently earned a Master of Forestry and Master of Business Administration from Yale, also came to Soul Fire to learn. He and Layel hit it off, and one evening, they wandered up the street from the farm to soak in a hot tub at a Buddhist temple.

That's where Layel shared their dream with Nikola: to create a safe, joyous space for Black and Indigenous communities in the forest. They'd take care of the trees, restore the land, and make art. This would be a place "to enrich the waterways, fill the food baskets, quicken the forests, rematriate laughter, paint a new culture, rewild our hearts, and heal our people, so that we may all be free."

Layel said that a couple of acres would be perfect to make this dream come true.

"What about closer to ten thousand acres, Layel?" Nikola asked.

10,000 acres is close to 7,600 football fields. It's more than 11 times the size of Central Park. Or 20 times the size of the country of Monaco!

As far-fetched as this sounded, however, Layel went with it. Nikola and Layel started to organize monthly meetings to envision this. They called it "Shelterwood."

Then all of a sudden, the pandemic hit. Still, as the world went into lockdown, Nikola and Layel moved forward with their dream.

"My co-founder and I were connected to a family who owns Leonard Lake Reserve," Layel says. "We entertained their motivations to transition the land in a partial discount sale to us. The motivation for the sale was due to wanting to reengage the land in a rightful relationship with Indigenous and Black communities. After a while, it became evident that this family was not ready to transition. . . . That's when we visited Camp Caz, a Christian camp owned by the United Church of Christ."

Layel got in touch with a family who had run a Christian camp in a forest in northern California for seventy-five years. They wanted to sell their land: nine hundred acres to be precise. "The property had just gone on the market, so we went to go see it."

They had some realtors on their side too. These were specialized real estate agents who work to decolonize real estate.

WHAT DOES "DECOLONIZING REAL ESTATE" MEAN?

To "decolonize" means to reexamine and make changes to counter the belief that the culture of a colonizing power is more worthy or important than the culture of a colonized people.

In other words, when it comes to real estate and land ownership, it means first acknowledging the colonial roots of real estate in the United States. Much of the owned land today is land that white people stole, displacing Black and Indigenous people who lived here.

Decolonization in real estate is a process of reckoning with the connection between wealth and the stolen wealth, land, and lives of Black and Indigenous peoples—and embracing the responsibility as white and non-Natives to repair this trauma by returning wealth, resources, and land back to the original peoples of the Americas.

One morning, Layel and Nikola drove past the Russian River and into the forest where some of the oldest redwood trees are home to spotted owls. They got out of the car and wandered through the beautiful nine hundred acres of land, taking in the flowing creek and blue sky.

The price? Four million dollars. How could they possibly come up with that much money?

That's when a Black artist, vocalist, and composer who prefers not to be named stepped in. This person offered a very generous grant that would help them with a down payment and start building Shelterwood.

One of the first things they did was invite local communities, which included Indigenous people in the hopes of building relationships with the Kashia and Southern Pomo tribes to connect and learn from them, which eventually happened.

"I really believe that in order for us to survive climate change, we need to learn how to change the story, how to position Black, Indigenous, Disabled, and Queer people at the front line, and to listen to what's going to work for them in order for us all to survive," Layel says. "I also believe that in order to change policy and economics, you have to do this through good storytelling."

Today, Layel describes Shelterwood as "a queer-centered stewardship project" and also "a disability justice organization." At the core is this belief: that you can make our ecosystem healthy again when you are in a deep relationship with the earth and with one another.

YOU CAN MAKE OUR ECOSYSTEM HEALTHY AGAIN WHEN YOU ARE IN A DEEP RELATIONSHIP WITH THE EARTH AND WITH ONE ANOTHER.

"In order for us to exist in any natural ecosystem, we need to know where our food is growing," Layel explains. They are learning about everything from how to tend a garden to how to do controlled burns on the land to manage the forest.

"If we can take our values and scale them one acre at a time, up to nine hundred acres, that resiliency is going to kind of reverberate beyond the forest edge, continue to create a better system for everyone," Layel says.

Layel is happily married to Shelterwood's community and retreat manager, Julia Velasquez. Their plan is to officially open a retreat center here to the public in 2027.

In addition to building a retreat center for people to come and connect with the land, they aim to organize other BIPOC communities toward land stewardship and changing culture to make more projects like theirs possible.

Layel often shares stories about how Black, Brown, and Indigenous people in marginal situations continue to thrive.

"I think one of the most important things for me at this moment is to remember that no matter what people have said to you, you are always a positive change for the planet. If you put your hands in the soil, smell the air, touch a tree, or pick a flower, then you can connect with the earth and make a positive change for her care."

YEMI AMU

FOUNDED: Oko Farms

WHERE: Brooklyn, New York

BEGINS HER DAY: making sure all her fish are alive

SPECIAL SAUCE: can grow food without soil!

INSTAGRAM: @okofarms

ONE WORD TO DESCRIBE YEMI: *daring*

WEBSITE: www.okofarms.org

PRONOUNS: she/they

Yemi Amu leaned over a very long plastic tank as a group of tilapia fish swam back and forth. Their iridescent blue-gray heads shimmered in the sunlight. Yemi scanned the water, looking for any fish that might be sick or stressed.

"Strong and healthy today!" Yemi said as her interns gathered round. Yemi noted this in her journal and peered in another tub, where plants sprouted up.

She spotted a beetle moseying up the stem of the watercress. "Flea beetle on the watercress!" Yemi announced. "Sorry little guy," Yemi said as she plucked the beetle off and dropped it into a small container.

You'd probably never expect to come across this huge, vibrant garden on the edge of a construction site in Brooklyn, New York. But that's Yemi for you: she had dreamed of creating an aquaponic farm in the middle of the city and made it a beautiful reality.

An "aquaponic farm" is when you grow fish and plants "together in a symbiotic ecosystem," Yemi explained.

Symbiotic means having a cooperative relationship. For example, if you have a dog, it depends on you to eat every day. And you depend on your dog for love.

An ecosystem is a community of organisms interacting in their environment. In Yemi's aquaponic farm ecosystem, these concepts are on display. First, the poop from all of these fish makes the plants grow. The plants have a big job too: they *purify* the water, which means they keep it clean. Finally, the microorganisms in the water break down the fish waste and turn it into nutrients to feed the plants.

But have you noticed something that's missing here on this farm? Soil! There's no soil at Oko Farms. *Oko* means "farm" in Yoruba, a language spoken in Nigeria, where Yemi was born and raised.

"It is a human right to be able to grow food for yourself," Yemi said on a PBS documentary. "To me, that's what aquaponics represents—this power and ability to feed yourself regardless of what your circumstances are."

In addition to watercress, Yemi grows peppers, okra, tomatoes, leeks, chives, onions, carrots, mint, basil, and more. Yemi moved to New York City when she was sixteen years old and often misses food from her home. So she also grows okra and green leafy vegetables to make her favorite Nigerian dishes.

WEST AFRICAN FLAVORS

Yemi loves planting West African veggies that she grew up with. There are lots of connections between her favorite foods and ones that you find in Caribbean and Asian cultures. This is because the British and other colonial powers stole seeds and people from different continents, moved them across oceans, and left behind crops that became staples across cultures. Peanuts, rice, corn, wheat, and yams all grow in West Africa. Let's take a look at some delicious dishes!

Did you know that eggplant is technically a fruit? In countries and territories in the Caribbean, such as St. Kitts and Nevis, Jamaica, and the US Virgin Islands, stewed or sauteed eggplant is often served with salt fish (codfish) and rice.

"In Nigeria, we have a category of 'swallows,'" Yemi says, explaining that these are "starchy, dough-like accompaniments to soups/stews." See page 122 for some yummy recipes from Yemi!

IT IS A HUMAN RIGHT TO BE ABLE TO GROW FOOD FOR YOURSELF

"A typical day for me is getting to the farm at 8:00 a.m. The first thing I do is walk through and make sure the fish and plants are doing well," Yemi said with a laugh.

That's why Yemi's assistants have notebooks. "I encourage journaling," Yemi said. "I ask, 'What do you see? What do you hear?' We use our senses and, based on our observations, we come up with a task list for the day."

Some days, everyone picks fresh veggies. Others, they seed new plants. Or look for pests eating the plants. If kids are visiting, Yemi might show them how to catch a fish and make fish tacos with fresh peppers.

Yemi said that she doesn't like to use sprays to kill the bugs because they "could also be harmful to the fish and to other beneficial insects that make up our ecosystem. We work really hard to do everything by hand, which is difficult. Also, you don't want to kill ladybugs or bees."

Yemi's farm is the first and only public aquaponics farm and education center in New York City. She donates about half of the food she grows to the community.

Just as importantly, Yemi educates people every week so they can grow their own food.

Yemi also visits schools to set up aquaponic systems in classrooms where kids raise goldfish and grow lettuce mixes to harvest and eat!

She often asks kids, "What does a farmer look like?"

They all say, "A guy in overalls." Yemi is showing the world this isn't true. She's showing everyone that she—and women who look like her—are real, hard-working farmers.

ACKNOWLEDGMENTS

To every woman in this book, I'm so grateful to you for trusting me, for opening up, and for inspiring me. Thank you to every farmer and food justice advocate I interviewed. You opened my eyes and lifted me up. You kept me going during the most overwhelming, anxious days.

My deepest gratitude goes to Leah Trotman, my incredible research assistant who showed up every week from London (as she completed her masters in Caribbean & Latin American Studies, and then from her home in the US Virgin Islands) with so much passion and enthusiasm.

I want to acknowledge the unnamed women—and men—who do the most difficult, longest, underpaid work on farms in the United States to feed people all over the world.

Also, Elizabeth Torres spent an afternoon with me to walk me through the lives and work of undocumented farmworkers (Ph.D. Sociology Student at UC Berkeley; Graduate Student Fellow at Berkeley Interdisciplinary Migration Initiative). She brought her baby, Oliver, to the interview that day!

All the hugs and kisses to my daughters Mae and Camille, such creative, brave, adventurous, nature-loving warriors in this big world.

A great appreciation to the amazing people at Little Bee Books for all of your thoughtful edits, design, illustrations, marketing, publicity, and more: Charlie Ilgunas, my editor, Steph Stilwell and Sydney Hackley, the designers of this book, Kristin Errico, copyeditor, and Paul Crichton and Maggie Salko in marketing and publicity.

An enormous thank you to Eric Myers, my agent, for being on my team and for correcting my dangling modifiers.

Thank you to my colleagues at RMI for cheering me on and supporting me. (Shoutouts to Matt Solomon, Leah Komos, Maddi Hall, Ali Hanson, Conrad Borges, Caroline Bennett, and Dina Cappiello!)

Big thanks to my brilliant and supportive writer-friends for being so generous and thoughtful, and also for keeping me accountable:

Alex Giardino
Angela Dalton
Mae Respicio
Suzanne LaFetra
Susie Meserve
Sharon Eberhardt
Laura Atkins
Amelinda Bérubé
Tamara Mahmood Hayes
Wendy McKee
Shellie Faught
Catey Miller
Melissa Mazzone
Bree Barton
Jacqueline Lipton
TJ Ohler
Alison Cherry
Ben LeRoy

A shout out to the mamas who continue to hold me and check in, my soul sisters:

Kellie Lund
Ariel Lustig
Elise Brewin
Desiree Ong
Arden Fredman
Siobhan van Winkel
Diane Friedlaender
Amanda Dora Riesman

Lastly, thank you to all of my kind, open-hearted readers, including children, parents, and teachers.

THANK YOU

Thank you for reading!

Turn the page to check out some tasty recipes!

RECIPES

OKRA SOUP AUTHOR: LOLA OSINKOLU

Okra soup is a very popular and delicious West African stew.

Prep Time: 10 minutes | **Cook Time:** 30 minutes | **Serves:** 6 people

INGREDIENTS

- Smoked turkey wings
- A pinch of salt
- 1 Tsp seasoning cube
- 1 small onion, minced
- 1 ½ lb Okra, half minced and half sliced
- 1 red bell pepper, minced
- 1 habanero pepper
- 3 Tbsp crayfish
- 4 Tbsp locust bean gum
- 1 large dry fish
- ½ to ¾ cup red palm oil or coconut oil
- 1 lb shrimp
- ½ lb spinach

INSTRUCTIONS

1. Boil the smoked turkey wings with salt, seasoning powder, and minced onions. Cook till tender.
2. While the meat is boiling, mince half the okra in a food processor or a chopper and slice the other half. Set aside.
3. Mince the red bell and habanero pepper in the chopper and set aside.
4. When the meat becomes tender, add the minced okra, pepper, crayfish, and locust bean, and leave to cook for about 10 minutes.
5. Shred and add the washed dry fish and let soften for about five minutes.
6. Add the palm oil, shrimp, and the minced and sliced okra. Leave to cook for about 3 to 5 minutes.
7. Stir in the spinach and mix until wilted.
8. Remove from heat immediately and serve.

NOTES

I like to mince half of the okra in a food chopper. This helps the okra develop that viscous consistency. If you want the okra soup to be more viscous, simply chop more than half of the okra.

The protein used is first boiled. The idea behind this is to create a base and stock for the soup.

It's advisable to boil meat till it's tender; also season moderately. It is essential to not overcook any vegetables. In this case, the Okra is cooked on medium heat to retain the nutrients, not burn it off with heat.

EFO RIRO AUTHOR: K'S CUISINE

This Nigerian vegetable soup is easy to make, delicious and nutritious. Efo can be paired with Nigerian swallows like eba, fufu, and amala or with rice, plantain, and other foods. This is the best efo riro recipe.

Prep Time: 10 minutes | **Cook Time:** 35 minutes

INGREDIENTS

- 12 oz beef and assorted meat
- 3 oz smoked fish
- 6 Scotch bonnet peppers (aka rodo peppers)
- 6 bell peppers
- 1 large onion
- 1 cup palm oil
- 2 stock cubes (any stock flavor)
- 4 Tbsp fermented locust beans (aka iru)
- ¼ lb prawns, fresh or dried
- 8 oz kale or any green leafy vegetable
- 9 oz spinach or any green leafy vegetable

INSTRUCTIONS

1. Boil the beef and assorted meat and set this aside.
2. Soak the smoked fish in hot salty water for 2 minutes (this removes the dirt off the fish), shred, and separate the bones from the fish.
3. Cut, wash, and, in another pot of boiling water, blanch the vegetables
4. Coarsely blend the Scotch bonnets, bell peppers, and onion in a food processor.
5. Place a large pot on the stove on medium heat and pour palm oil into the pot. When palm oil is heated, add the blended peppers, stock cubes, and locust beans, and leave to cook for 10 minutes.
6. Add in boiled beef, assorted meats, and dry fish. Add salt to taste.
7. Leave to cook for another 10–15 minutes. By now the stew should be fried and thick in consistency. The stew should not be watery.
8. Add the blanched vegetables and stir them in the stew. Leave to simmer on low heat for 2 minutes. Do not overcook the vegetable as this would mean the vegetables are losing most of their nutrients.
9. Take off heat and serve.
10. Enjoy efo riro with any swallow*, like eba, amala, pounded yam or rice, plantain, or any food of choice.

* Nigerian swallows are starchy, dough-like balls, small enough to "swallow," and usually accompany soups.

AMALA AND EWEDU SOUP AUTHOR: CHEF'S PENCIL STAFF

A beloved Nigerian dish cherished by the Yoruba community. The distinctive flavor of this meal is derived from the combination of Ewedu leaves and Amala.

Prep Time: 15 minutes | **Cook Time:** 15 minutes | **Servings:** 4

INGREDIENTS

- 1 big bunch of ewedu leaves
- 2 cups water
- 1 Tbsp fermented locust beans (aka iru)
- 1 Tbsp ground crayfish (heaped)
- ½ Maggi crayfish flavored bouillon cube
- ½ any preferred flavored bouillon cube
- Salt to taste

For Amala:

- 2 cups yam flour
- 2 cups water

INSTRUCTIONS

1. Thoroughly wash the ewedu leaves, and remove and discard the tough stems.
2. Add the leaves and 2 cups of water to a medium-sized pot, and bring to a boil. When the leaves are cooked, take them off the heat to cool a bit, then use a mortar and pestle to pound the leaves along with the locust beans.*
3. Transfer the ewedu to a pan and add the crayfish, the bouillon cube, and salt to your liking. Mix everything well and heat it through, then turn off the heat and let it sit for 3 minutes to steam, stirring occasionally. Do not overcook the mixture or the ewedu will go brown.

How to Make Amala:

1. Add 2 cups of water to a medium pot and bring it to a rolling boil. Add the yam flour gradually, stirring continuously to break any lumps that might form.
2. Adjust the consistency with more flour (if too thin) or more water (if too thick).
3. Stir vigorously, cover with a lid, and cook for 10 minutes until firm.
4. Let the amala cool, and form balls in your hands. Wrap them up in plastic wrap.
5. Serve the delicious ewedu soup with amala and enjoy!

* Alternatively, you can add the cooked leaves and locust beans to a blender along with about 1/2 cup of the cooking water from the leaves and pulse-blitz to a smooth puree. Add the water gradually to make sure it's not too watery.

RESOURCES

ORGANIZATIONS:

Organizations such as Agrarian Trust and Northeast Farmers of Color Land Trust are working tirelessly to offer land leases and additional resources to Black farmers interested in acquiring land. Black to the Land Coalition is most interested in providing "meaningful outdoor experiences" for BIPOC communities, further strengthening connections to the land, a welcome development after centuries of long-discrimination against Black farmers. Below are various other organizations dedicated to similar goals, many of which are mentioned throughout this book.

African American Museum and Library at Oakland (AAMLO)
Agrarian Trust
Agriculture and Land-based Training Association (ALBA)
Alianza Nacional de Campesinas
Alliance for Fair Food
American Farmland Trust
Berkeley Food Institute
Black to the Land Coalition
Coalition of Immokalee Workers
Community Alliance with Family Farmers (CAFF)
Detroit Black Farmer Land Fund
The Edible Schoolyard Project
Fair Food Program
Farms to Grow
Farmworker Justice
Feeding America
Food Culture Collective
Freedom Farmers' Market
Gill Tract Community Farm
Global Growers Network
Justice for Migrant Women
Keep Growing Detroit
Líderes Campesinas
Mandela Grocery Cooperative
Northeast Farmers of Color Land Trust
Pineros Y Campesinos Unidos del Noroeste (PCUN)
RAFI
United Farm Workers
United States Department of Agriculture (USDA)
World Central Kitchen

MEDIA:

Watch

Leah Penniman's TED Talk about "Farming While Black."
https://www.youtube.com/watch?v=9QYDXtMiV8o

Hungry for Change, a short film made by the Berkeley Food Institute at UC Berkeley. It features twenty trailblazing food systems reformers from California, dedicated to advancing equity, health, and sustainability in food and farming systems.

The "The Black Panthers: Free Breakfast Program" on PBS.
https://www.pbs.org/video/independent-lens-free-breakfast-program/

Joanna Letz on Bluma Flower Farms on *Farm Dreams*, Season 1, Episode 2 available on Disney+

Food Chains documentary
This film focuses on farmworker injustice—and how farmworkers have organized to petition for better pay. In the film, you also get to meet The Coalition of Immokalee Workers (see page 53-57).
https://rocofilms.com/films/food-chains/

Dolores, a documentary about activist Dolores Huerta, who tirelessly led the fight for racial and labor justice.
https://www.pbs.org/independentlens/documentaries/dolores-huerta/

A 1-minute video about the Fair Food Program.
https://fairfoodprogram.org/

By harnessing the power of consumer demand, the Fair Food Program gives farmworkers a voice in the decisions that affect their lives and prevents the abuses that have plagued agriculture for generations.

Also, the documentary *Food, Inc. 2* features the Fair Food Program
https://www.magpictures.com/foodinc2/screenings/

Homegrown
Atlanta-based farmer and food activist Jamila Norman helps home-owners transform their yards into urban farms while discussing the many benefits that farms and gardens can bring to communities.
https://www.youtube.com/watch?v=uFz3OFs72Dc&t=6s

Common Ground. Free to educators.

"Solutions to our climate crisis and addressing topics such as Regeneration, Social Justice, Food Sovereignty, and Politics. includes a free curriculum for educators."

https://commongroundfilm.org/education/

More about Alice Waters and The Edible Schoolyard on PBS:

Visit a schoolyard garden and kitchen project in Berkeley started by restauranteur Alice Waters in an effort to connect students to the land. How the city of Stockton turned around its dismal graduation rate, the accuracy of dropout rates, and a unique summer camp run by a Northern California school district for more than half a century."

https://www.pbssocal.org/shows/inside-california-education/episodes/inside-california-education-edible-schoolyard

"Alice Waters's Edible Schoolyard Project has been cultivating minds and fostering community worldwide for 25 years."

https://www.pbs.org/video/edible-classroom-21ObbR/

Listen

Camille Dungy on NPR radio, "She ripped up her manicured lawn and challenged the norms of gardening stories."

https://www.npr.org/2023/05/05/1172727763/garden-gardening-book-writing-soil-dungy

The story of Ruth Beckford's life and the Free Breakfast for School Children Program at KQED radio.

https://www.kqed.org/arts/13950520/ruth-beckford-dance-black-panthers-free-breakfast-program

Shreya Ramachandran in a documentary called *Feast or Famine: California's Water Crisis*. It explores when California transitioned from a drought-stricken state to having too much water with nowhere to go.

https://www.youtube.com/watch?v=IzIb17uJtMU

The story about Lupe Gonzalo on the *Good Night Stories for Rebel Girls Podcast*

https://www.rebelgirls.com/podcast/lupe-gonzalo-sowing-seeds-of-change

GLOSSARY

Agrifood: the commercial production of food by farming

Agroecology: farming in ways that work more closely with nature, plants, animals, people, and their environment; it usually includes limiting the use of chemicals to grow food

Aquaponic: a system of growing plants in water that is also used to cultivate aquatic organisms such as fish

Biodiversity: biological diversity among and within plant and animal species in an environment

Climate crisis: Since the Industrial Revolution, human activity has caused the earth to heat up. Unfortunately, rising temperatures don't really mean that we'll have nicer weather. The changing climate is making our weather more extreme and unpredictable. Some of the hottest years have happened in the past twenty years.

Cultural Anthropologist: someone who studies living societies—what makes them similar to and different from each other

Decolonize: to reexamine and make changes to counter the belief that the culture of a colonizing power is more worthy or important than the culture of a colonized people

Environmental Justice: the idea that everyone—regardless of race, color, origin, disability, or income—has the right to the same environmental protections and benefits, as well as meaningful involvement in the policies that shape their communities

Food apartheid: the racist and oppressive systems that create inequitable food environments

Food desert: a neighborhood or community where healthy, affordable food is difficult to obtain

Food sovereignty: the right of peoples to healthy and culturally appropriate food produced through ecologically sound and sustainable methods, and their right to define their own food and agriculture systems

Heat Waves: a period of abnormally hot and usually humid weather

Intersectional agriculture: the examination of how growing food crosses with another concept, such as race, gender, disability, sexuality, or other

Permaculture: when you manage land in ways that mimic healthy natural ecosystems, regenerative agriculture, rewilding, and sustainable agriculture

Symbiotic ecosystem: a community of organisms that have a cooperative relationship with other organisms in their environment

Tenant farmer: someone who grows crops on land that's owned by someone else

PHOTO CREDITS

Photos by 96, 97, 98 - Ana Elisa Pérez Quintero; 72, 75 - Adrionna Fike; 60, 63 - Amber Bell; 44, 45, 46 - Bianca Datta; 109 - Caitlin Joseph; 84, 85 - Dr. Gail Myers; 88, 89, 90, 91 - Elizabeth Couse; 36 - H. Nieto-Friga; vi, 2, 4 - Ivy Walls; 6 - Jamel Mosely; 30 - Kanchan Dawn Hunter; 104, 105, 107, 108 - Katie Willis; 78, 80, 81, 83 - Katie Willis; 110, 112, 115 - Layel Camargo and Julia Velasquez; 68 - Liz Birnbaum; 9 - Montana Monardes; 100, 102, 103 - Paige Green; 58 - Rebecca Som Castellano; 18, 19, 22, 23 - Saara Nafici; 40 - Sheila Tupua-Sulu; 92 - Shreya Ramachandran; 12, 13, 15, 16 - Suzanne Willow and Lanita Witt; 24, 25, 27 - Tepfirah Rushdan; 116 - Yemi Amu; iStock: 48 - alexeys, 36, 72 - alicjane, 92 - alvarez, 30, 60 - ANA LEBIODIENE, 6 - anilakkus, 72 - annaratner, 72, 74 - AnnaStills, 58 - Anton Skripachev, vi - ArtCookStudio, 36 - audaxl, 48, 116 - BasieB, 55 - batuhan toker, 37 - Biserka Stojanovic, 48 - branex, 72 - BruceBlock, 52 - Carlos Aguirre, iv, 58, 64 - cturtletrax, 47 - dareknie, 34 - DianeBentleyRaymond, 30 - digihelion, 76 - DimaSobko, 68 - dulvet, 58 - dogayusufdokdok, 51 - Drazen Zigic, vi - DutchScenery, 52 - Dvoinik, 110 - elenaleonova, 110 - espiegle, 64 - eurobanks, 6, 93, 110 - Evgeny Shaplov, 42 - fcafotodigital, 35 - Fly View Productions, 6 - fokkebok, 44 - Fotofreak75, 92 - Francesco Scabar, 40 - Gassenee Tiwwong, 28 - ggutarin, vi, 52 - GneshYeh, 5, 32 - Goodboy Picture Company, 40 - guenterguni, 84 - howtogoto, 36, 92 - ideeone, 39 - Imagine Saturations, 52 - JackF, 30 - Jana Milin, 64, 67 - Jan Ziegler, 117 - josefkubes, 72 - Juhla, 36 - Juniper_Berry, 64 - Jurgute, 8 - justhavealook, 64 - karandaev, 113 - kata716, 116 - lena_volo, 68 - Leonsbox, 30 - littlekiss photography, 118 - los_angela, 116 - LUNAMARINA, 68 - Maryviolet, 9 - mediaphotos, 44, 116 - mgstudyo, 52 - MRaust, 6 - Neyya, 52 - NikonShutterman, 48 - nzfhatipoglu, 65 - PeopleImages, vi, 116 - photosbyjimn, 40 - pressdigital, 110 - ProfessionalStudioImages, 72 - querbeet, 41, 72, 92, 116 - RachelDewis, 48 - redstallion, 40, 110 - rudolfgeiger, 35 - RyanJLane, 36 - sandsun, 58 - Sasithorn Phuapankasemsuk, 94 - schulzie, 68 - seagames50, 64 - Serg_Velusceac, 58 - simonkr, 30, 64 - southtownboy, 68 - SteafPong88, 30 - Sundry Photography, 92 - temmuzcan, spine - Tim UR, spine - valentinarr, 40 - Valeriy_G, spine - Viktar, 6, 11 - xavierarnau, 92 - xijian, 36 - yanikap, 52 - ZoiaKostina

BIBLIOGRAPHY

Aghomo, Oisakhose. "Forging Pathways to Land Access for BIPOC Farmers in Georgia." *Civil Eats*, March 2, 2023. https://civileats.com/2023/03/02/forging-pathways-to-land-access-for-bipoc-farmers-in-georgia/

Aguirre, Fabián and Maya Pisciotto. *Hungry For Change: California's Emerging Food Systems Leaders*. Berkeley Food Institute, June 21, 2018. https://www.youtube.com/watch?v=wRDFCHOeuJ4

Block, Melissa. "She ripped up her manicured lawn and challenged the norms of gardening stories." *NPR*, May 5, 2023. https://www.npr.org/2023/05/05/1172727763/garden-gardening-book-writing-soil-dungy

Bratt, Peter, dir. *Dolores*. Independent Lens film, 2018. https://www.pbs.org/independentlens/documentaries/dolores-huerta/

Bustillo, Ximena. "'Rampant issues': Black farmers are still left out at USDA." *Politico*, July 5, 2021. https://www.politico.com/news/2021/07/05/black-farmers-left-out-usda-497876

Bustillo, Ximena. "In 2022, Black farmers were persistently left behind from the USDA's loan system." *NPR*, February 19, 2023. https://www.npr.org/2023/02/19/1156851675/in-2022-black-farmers-were-persistently-left-behind-from-the-usdas-loan-system

Catalan, Maria. "From Farmworker to Farm Owner." TEDx Fruitvale, Oakland, CA, October 14, 2011. Video, 7 min., 45 sec. https://www.youtube.com/watch?v=V21JiiP-CvI

Cather, Alexina. "40 Under 40: The Rising Stars in New York City Food Policy." Hunter College New York City Food Policy Center, May 19, 2017. https://www.nycfoodpolicy.org/2017-40-40/

Dhanesha, Neel. "The wasted potential of garbage dumps." *Vox*, October 24, 2022. https://www.vox.com/the-highlight/23377770/garbage-dump-landfill-solar-climate-justice-sunnyside-ira

Dreier, Hannah. "Biden Administration Plans Crackdown on Migrant Child Labor." *New York Times*, February 28, 2023. https://www.nytimes.com/2023/02/27/us/biden-child-labor.html?unlocked_article_code=1.FU4.Okdr.aC-eJxZQe2so&smid=url-share#

Dungy, Camille T. *Soil: The Story of a Black Mother's Garden*. Simon & Schuster, 2023.

Gebreyesus, Ruth. "'One of the biggest, baddest things we did': Black Panthers' free breakfasts, 50 years on." *The Guardian*, October 18, 2019. https://www.theguardian.com/us-news/2019/oct/17/black-panther-party-oakland-free-breakfast-50th-anniversary

Haas, Michaela. "Healing the Land and Themselves." *YES!*, December 29, 2022. https://www.yesmagazine.org/environment/2022/12/29/land-black-indigenous-farming

Harris-Perry, Melissa. "The Fight For The Survival of Black Farmers." *The Takeaway*. Podcast. WNYC Studios, March 6, 2023. https://www.wnycstudios.org/podcasts/takeaway/segments/fight-survival-black-farmers

Jordan, Miriam. "Farmworkers, Mostly Undocumented, Become 'Essential' During Pandemic." *New York Times*, April 2, 2020. https://www.nytimes.com/2020/04/02/us/coronavirus-undocumented-immigrant-farmworkers-agriculture.html?unlocked_article_code=1.7E0.ARQR.Ba2HrikQkRAz&smid=url-share#

Kimmerer, Robin Wall. *Braiding Sweetgrass: Indigenous Wisdom, Scientific Knowledge and the Teachings of Plants*. Milkweed Editions, 2015.

Li, Chloe K., producer. "How are Black American farmers reclaiming their land?" The Take by *Al Jazeera*, September 21, 2022. Podcast, 19 min., 18 sec. https://www.aljazeera.com/podcasts/2022/9/21/how-are-black-american-farmers-reclaiming-their-land

Liang Chang, Vera. "Meet the Farmworkers Leading the #MeToo Fight for Workers Everywhere." *KQED*, May 25, 2018. https://www.kqed.org/bayareabites/128564/meet-the-farmworkers-leading-the-metoo-fight-for-workers-everywhere

Madrigal, Alexis. "KQED Youth Takeover: Four Stewards at Work Healing Their Land and Communities." *KQED*, April 28, 2023. https://www.kqed.org/forum/2010101892985/kqed-youth-takeover-four-stewards-at-work-healing-their-land-and-communities

Myers, Gail. Rhythms of the Land. Farms To Grow, Inc., 2022.

Nelson, Stanley, dir. "The Black Panthers: Free Breakfast Program." Clip excerpt from *The Black Panthers: Vanguard of the Revolution*, Independent Lens film, 2016. https://www.pbs.org/video/independent-lens-free-breakfast-program/

Nieves, Evelyn. "Accord With Tomato Pickers Ends Boycott Of Taco Bell." *Washington Post*, March 8, 2005. https://www.washingtonpost.com/archive/politics/2005/03/09/accord-with-tomato-pickers-ends-boycott-of-taco-bell/b3cc421a-33ad-4f0e-80ba-8f570e5bae1d/

Officinalis, Indy. *Farm Dreams*. National Geographic series, 2023.

Penniman, Leah. "Black Farmers Are Embracing Climate-Resilient Farming." *Civil Eats*, January 20, 2020. https://civileats.com/2020/01/20/black-farmers-are-embracing-climate-resilient-farming/

Penniman, Leah. *Black Earth Wisdom: Soulful Conversations with Black Environmentalists*. Amistad, 2023.

Penniman, Leah. "Farming While Black." TED Talk, Boston, MA, Jan 18, 2023. Video, 11 min., 13 sec. https://www.youtube.com/watch?v=9QYDXtMiV8o

Penniman, Leah. *Farming While Black: Soul Fire Farm's Practical Guide to Liberation on the Land*. Chelsea Green Publishing, 2018.

Ramchandani, Ariel. "There's a Sexual-Harassment Epidemic on America's Farms." *The Atlantic*, January 29, 2018. https://www.theatlantic.com/business/archive/2018/01/agriculture-sexual-harassment/550109/

Ranwal, Sanjay. *Food Chains: The Revolution in America's Fields*. Screen Media Films, 2014.

Ríos Treviño, Lorena. "These Families Lead Double Lives Across the U.S. Mexican Border." *National Geographic*, October 10, 2022. https://www.nationalgeographic.com/history/article/these-families-lead-double-lives-across-the-us-mexico-border

Robinson, Samuel. "Detroit hires first urban agriculture director." *Axios Detroit*, September 12, 2023. https://www.axios.com/local/detroit/2023/09/12/detroit-first-urban-agriculture-director-tepfirah-rushdan

Soul Fire Farms. *Liberation on Land* skillshare video series. Last updated July 31, 2024. https://www.youtube.com/playlist?list=PLR9X2SVBYFDJnPQXceKROkAuh-xXt2_um

Sewell, Summer. "There were nearly a million black farmers in 1920. Why have they disappeared?" *The Guardian*, April 29, 2019. https://www.theguardian.com/environment/2019/apr/29/why-have-americas-black-farmers-disappeared

Tickell, Josh and Rebecca, dirs. *Common Ground*. Big Picture Ranch, 2024.

USDA Economic Research Service. "Legal Status and Migration Practices of Hired Crop Farmworkers." Farm Labor. Accessed September 5, 2024. https://www.ers.usda.gov/topics/farm-economy/farm-labor/#legalstatus

Walker, Nani. *Alice Waters: How to Start a Food Revolution*. LA Times Studios, 2021.

Wiessner, Daniel. "Raisin company pays $2 mln to settle EEOC claims over farmworker harassment." *Reuters*, March 12, 2024. https://www.reuters.com/legal/government/raisin-company-pays-2-mln-settle-eeoc-claims-over-farmworker-harassment-2024-03-12/

Wood, Cirrus. "East Bay food-justice movement has deep roots in Black Panther Party." *NOSH*, August 24, 2017. https://www.berkeleyside.org/2017/08/24/east-bay-food-justice-black-panther-party

INDEX